THE COMPLETE EPIC OF
GILGAMESH

BY
LEONIDAS LE CENCI HAMILTON

pac ps
Pacific Publishing Studio

CONTENTS

ALCOVE I

ALCOVE II

ALCOVE I

TABLET I

COLUMN I

INVOCATION

O LOVE, my queen and goddess, come to me;
My soul shall never cease to worship thee;
Come pillow here thy head upon my breast,
And whisper in my lyre thy softest, best,
And sweetest melodies of bright *Sami*,
Our Happy Fields above dear *Subartu*;
Come nestle closely with those lips of love
And balmy breath, and I with thee shall rove
Through *Sari* past ere life on earth was known,
And Time unconscious sped not, nor had flown.
Thou art our all in this impassioned life:
How sweetly comes thy presence ending strife,
Thou god of peace and Heaven's undying joy,
Oh, hast thou ever left one pain or cloy
Upon this beauteous world to us so dear?
To all mankind thou art their goddess here.
To thee we sing, our holiest, fairest god,
The One who in that awful chaos trod
And woke the Elements by Law of Love
To teeming worlds in harmony to move.
From chaos thou hast led us by thy hand,
  Thus spoke to man upon that budding land:
"The Queen of Heaven, of the dawn am I,
The goddess of all wide immensity,

For thee I open wide the golden gate
Of happiness, and for thee love create
To glorify the heavens and fill with joy
The earth, its children with sweet love employ."
Thou gavest then the noblest melody
And highest bliss--grand nature's harmony.
With love the finest particle is rife,
And deftly woven in the woof of life,
In throbbing dust or clasping grains of sand,
In globes of glistening dew that shining stand
On each pure petal, Love's own legacies
Of flowering verdure, Earth's sweet panoplies;
By love those atoms sip their sweets and pass
To other atoms, join and keep the mass
With mighty forces moving through all space,
'Tis thus on earth all life has found its place.
Through Kisar, Love came formless through the air
In countless forms behold her everywhere!
Oh, could we hear those whispering roses sweet,
Three beauties bending till their petals meet,
And blushing, mingling their sweet fragrance there
In language yet unknown to mortal ear.
Their whisperings of love from morn till night
Would teach us tenderly to love the right.
O Love, here stay! Let chaos not return!
With hate each atom would its lover spurn
In air above, on land, or in the sea,
O World, undone and lost that loseth thee!
For love we briefly come, and pass away
For other men and maids; thus bring the day
Of love continuous through this glorious life.
Oh, hurl away those weapons fierce of strife!
We here a moment, point of time but live,
Too short is life for throbbing hearts to grieve.
Thrice holy is that form that love hath kissed,
And happy is that man with heart thus blessed.
Oh, let not curses fall upon that head
Whom love hath cradled on the welcome bed

Of bliss, the bosom of our fairest god,
Or hand of love e'er grasp the venging rod.

Oh, come, dear Zir-ri, tune your lyres and lutes,
And sing of love with chastest, sweetest notes,
Of Accad's goddess Ishtar, Queen of Love,
And Izdubar, with softest measure move;
Great Samas' son, of him dear Zir-ri sing!
Of him whom goddess Ishtar warmly wooed,
Of him whose breast with virtue was imbued.
He as a giant towered, lofty grown,

As Babil's great *pa-te-si* was he known,
His armèd fleet commanded on the seas
And erstwhile travelled on the foreign leas;
His mother Ellat-gula on the throne
From Erech all Kardunia ruled alone.

COLUMN II

THE FALL OF ERECH

O Moon-god, hear my cry! With thy pure light
Oh, take my spirit through that awful night
That hovers o'er the long-forgotten years,
To sing Accadia's songs and weep her tears!
'Twas thus I prayed, when lo! my spirit rose
On fleecy clouds, enwrapt in soft repose;
And I beheld beneath me nations glide
In swift succession by, in all their pride:
The earth was filled with cities of mankind,
And empires fell beneath a summer wind.
The soil and clay walked forth upon the plains
In forms of life, and every atom gains
A place in man or breathes in animals;
And flesh and blood and bones become the walls

Of palaces and cities, which soon fall
To unknown dust beneath some ancient wall.
All this I saw while guided by the stroke
Of unseen pinions:
                    Then amid the smoke
That rose o'er burning cities, I beheld
White Khar-sak-kur-ra's brow arise that held
The secrets of the gods--that felt the prore
Of Khasisadra's ark; I heard the roar
Of battling elements, and saw the waves
That tossed above mankind's commingled graves.
The mighty mountain as some sentinel
Stood on the plains alone; and o'er it fell
A halo, bright, divine; its summit crowned
With sunbeams, shining on the earth around
And o'er the wide expanse of plains;--below
Lay Khar-sak-kal-ama with light aglow,
And nestling far away within my view
Stood Erech, Nipur, Marad, Eridu,
And Babylon, the tower-city old,
In her own splendor shone like burnished gold.

And lo! grand Erech in her glorious days
Lies at my feet. I see a wondrous maze
Of vistas, groups, and clustering columns round,
Within, without the palace;--from the ground
Of outer staircases, massive, grand,
Stretch to the portals where the pillars stand.
A thousand carvèd columns reaching high
To silver rafters in an azure sky,
And palaces and temples round it rise
With lofty turrets glowing to the skies,
And massive walls far spreading o'er the plains,
Here live and move Accadia's courtly trains,
And see! the *pit-u-dal-ti* at the gates,
And *masari* patrol and guard the streets!

And yonder comes a *kis-ib*, nobleman,
With a young prince; and see! a caravan
Winds through the gates! With men the streets are filled!
And chariots, a people wise and skilled
In things terrestrial, what science, art,
Here reign! With laden ships from every mart
The docks are filled, and foreign fabrics bring
From peoples, lands, where many an empire, king,
Have lived and passed away, and naught have left
In. history or song. Dread Time hath cleft
Us far apart; their kings and kingdoms, priests
And bards are gone, and o'er them sweep the mists
Of darkness backward spreading through all time,
Their records swept away in every clime.
Those alabaster stairs let us ascend,
And through this lofty portal we will wend.
See! richest Sumir rugs amassed, subdue
The tilèd pavement with its varied hue,
Upon the turquoise ceiling sprinkled stars
Of gold and silver crescents in bright pairs!
And gold-fringed scarlet curtains grace each door,
And from the inlaid columns reach the floor:
From golden rods extending round the halls,
Bright silken hangings drape the sculptured walls.

But part those scarlet hangings at the door
Of yon grand chamber! tread the antique floor!
Behold the sovereign on her throne of bronze,
While crouching at her feet a lion fawns;
The glittering court with gold and gems ablaze
With ancient splendor of the glorious days
Of Accad's sovereignty. Behold the ring
Of dancing beauties circling while they sing
With amorous forms in moving melody,
The measure keep to music's harmony.

Hear! how the music swells from silver lute
And golden-stringèd lyres and softest flute
And harps and tinkling cymbals, measured drums,
While a soft echo from the chamber comes.

But see! the sovereign lifts her jewelled hand,
The music ceases at the Queen's command;
And lo! two chiefs in warrior's array,
With golden helmets plumed with colors gay,
And golden shields, and silver coats of mail,
Obeisance make to her with faces pale,
Prostrate themselves before their sovereign's throne;
In silence brief remain with faces prone,
Till Ellat-gula speaks: "My chiefs, arise!
What word have ye for me? what new surprise?
Tur-tau-u, rising, says, "O Dannat Queen!
Thine enemy, Khum-baba with Rim-siu
With clanging shields, appears upon the hills,
And Elam's host the land of Sumir fills."
"Away, ye chiefs! sound loud the *nappa-khu*!
Send to their post each warrior bar-ru!"
The gray embattlements rose in the light
That lingered yet from Samas' rays, ere Night
Her sable folds had spread across the sky.
Thus Erech stood, where in her infancy
The huts of wandering Accads had been built
Of soil, and rudely roofed by woolly pelt
O'erlaid upon the shepherd's worn-out staves,
And yonder lay their fathers' unmarked graves.
Their chieftains in those early days oft meet
Upon the mountains where they Samas greet,
With their rude sacrifice upon a tree
High-raised that their sun-god may shilling see
Their offering divine; invoking pray
For aid, protection, blessing through the day.

Beneath these walls and palaces abode
The spirit of their country--each man trod
As if his soul to Erech's weal belonged,
And heeded not the enemy which thronged
Before the gates, that now were closed with bars
Of bronze thrice fastened.

                          See the thousand cars
And chariots arrayed across the plains!
The marching hosts of Elam's armèd trains,
The archers, slingers in advance amassed,
With black battalions in the centre placed,
With chariots before them drawn in line,

Bedecked with brightest trappings iridine.,
While gorgeous plumes of Elam's horses nod
Beneath the awful sign of Elam's god.
On either side the mounted spearsmen far
Extend; and all the enginery of war
Are brought around the walls with fiercest shouts,
And from behind their shields each archer shoots.

Thus Erech is besieged by her dread foes,
And she at last must feel Accadia's woes,
And feed the vanity of conquerors,
Who boast o'er victories in all their wars.
Great Subartu has fallen by Sutu
And Kassi, Goim fell with Lul-lu-bu,
Thus Khar-sak-kal-a-ma all Eridu
O'erran with Larsa's allies; Subartu
With Duran thus was conquered by these sons
Of mighty Shem and strewn was Accad's bones
Throughout her plains, and mountains, valleys fair,
Unburied lay in many a wolf's lair.

Oh, where is Accad's chieftain Izdubar,
Her mightiest unrivalled prince of war?

The turrets on the battlemented walls
Swarm with skilled bowmen, archers--from them falls
A cloud of wingèd missiles on their foes,
Who swift reply with shouts and twanging bows;
And now amidst the raining death appears
The scaling ladder, lined with glistening spears,
But see! the ponderous catapults now crush
The ladder, spearsmen, with their mighty rush
Of rocks and beams, nor in their fury slacked
As if a toppling wall came down intact
Upon the maddened mass of men below.
But other ladders rise, and up them flow
The tides of armèd spearsmen with their shields;
From others bowmen shoot, and each man wields,
A weapon, never yielding to his foe,
For death alone he aims with furious blow.
At last upon the wall two soldiers spring,
A score of spears their corses backward fling.
But others take their place, and man to man,
And spear to spear, and sword to sword, till ran
The walls with slippery gore; but Erech's men
Are brave and hurl them from their walls again.
And now the battering-rams with swinging power
Commence their thunders, shaking every tower;
And miners work beneath the crumbling walls,

Alas! before her foemen Erech falls.
Vain are suspended chains against the blows
Of dire assaulting engines.
                              Ho! there goes
The eastern wall with Erech's strongest tower!
And through the breach her furious foemen pour:
A wall of steel withstands the onset fierce,
But thronging Elam's spears the lines soon pierce,
A band of chosen men there fight to die,
Before their enemies disdain to fly;
The masari within the breach thus died,

And with their dying shout the foe defied.
The foes swarm through the breach and o'er the walls,
And Erech in extremity loud calls
Upon the gods for aid, but prays for naught,
While Elam's soldiers, to a frenzy wrought,
Pursue and slay, and sack the city old
With fiendish shouts for blood and yellow gold.
Each man that falls the foe decapitates,
And bears the reeking death to Erech's gates.
The gates are hidden 'neath the pile of heads
That climbs above the walls, and outward spreads
A heap of ghastly plunder bathed in blood.
Beside them calm scribes of the victors stood,
And careful note the butcher's name, and check
The list; and for each head a price they make.
Thus pitiless the sword of Elam gleams
And the best blood of Erech flows in streams.
From Erech's walls some fugitives escape,
And others in Euphrates wildly leap,
And hide beneath its rushes on the bank
And many 'neath the yellow waters sank.

The harper of the Queen, an agèd man,
Stands lone upon the bank, while he doth scan
The horizon with anxious, careworn face,
Lest ears profane of Elam's hated race
Should hear his strains of mournful melody:
Now leaning on his harp in memory
Enwrapt, while fitful breezes lift his locks
Of snow, he sadly kneels upon the rocks
And sighing deeply clasps his hands in woe,
While the dread past before his mind doth flow.
A score and eight of years have slowly passed
Since Rim-a-gu, with Elam's host amassed,
Kardunia's ancient capital had stormed.
The glorious walls and turrets are transformed
To a vast heap of ruins, weird, forlorn,

And Elam's spears gleam through the coming morn.
From the sad sight his eyes he turns away,

His soul breathes through his harp while he doth play
With bended head his agèd hands thus woke
The woes of Erech with a measured stroke:

O Erech! dear Erech, my beautiful home,
  Accadia's pride, O bright land of the bard,
Come back to my vision, dear Erech, oh, come!
  Fair land of my birth, how thy beauty is marred!
The horsemen of Elam, her spearsmen and bows,
  Thy treasures have ravished, thy towers thrown down,
And Accad is fallen, trod down by her foes.
  Oh, where are thy temples of ancient renown?

Gone are her brave heroes beneath the red tide,
  Gone are her white vessels that rode o'er the main,
No more on the river her pennon shall ride,
  Gargan-na is fallen, her people are slain.
Wild asses shall gallop across thy grand floors,
  And wild bulls shall paw them and hurl the dust high
Upon the wild cattle that flee through her doors,
  And doves shall continue her mournful slave's cry.

Oh, where are the gods of our Erech so proud,
  As flies they are swarming away from her halls,
The Sedu of Erech are gone as a cloud,
  As wild fowl are flying away from her walls.
Three years did she suffer, besieged by her foes,
  Her gates were thrown down and defiled by the feet
Who brought to poor Erech her tears and her woes,
  In vain to our Ishtar with prayers we entreat.

To Ishtar bowed down doth our Bel thus reply,
  "Come, Ishtar, my queenly one, hide all thy tears,
Our hero, Tar-u-man-i izzu Sar-ri,
  In Kipur is fortified with his strong spears.

The hope of Kardunia, land of my delight,
  Shall come to thy rescue, upheld by my hands,
Deliverer of peoples, whose heart is aright,
  Protector of temples, shall lead his brave bands.

Awake then, brave Accad, to welcome the day!
  Behold thy bright banners yet flaming on high,
Triumphant are streaming on land and the sea!
  Arise, then, O Accad! behold the Sami!

Arranged in their glory the mighty gods come
In purple and gold the grand Tam-u doth shine
Over Erech, mine Erech, my beautiful home,
Above thy dear ashes, behold thy god's sign!

COLUMN III

THE RESCUE OF ERECH BY IZDUBAR

Heabani, weary, eyes his native land,
And on his harp now lays his trembling hand;
The song has ended in a joyous lay,
And yet, alas! his hands but sadly play:
Unused to hope, the strings refuse their aid
To tune in sympathy, and heartless played.
Again the minstrel bows his head in woe,
And the hot tear-drops from his eyelids flow,
And chanting now a mournful melody,
O'er Erech's fall, thus sang an elegy:

"How long, O Ishtar, will thy face be turned,
While Erech desolate doth cry to thee?
Thy towers magnificent, oh, hast thou spurned?
Her blood like water in Ul-bar, oh, see!
The seat of thine own oracle behold!
The fire hath ravaged all thy cities grand,
And like the showers of Heaven them all doth fold.
O Ishtar! broken-hearted do I stand!

Oh, crush our enemies as yonder reed!
For hopeless, lifeless, kneels thy bard to thee,
And, oh! I would exalt thee in my need,
From thy resentment, anger, oh, us free!

With eyes bedimmed with tears, he careful scans
The plain, "Perhaps the dust of caravans
It is! But no!! I see long lines of spears!
A warrior from the lifting cloud appears,
And chariots arrayed upon the plain!
And is the glorious omen not in vain?
What! no?" He rubs his eyes in wild surprise,
And drinks the vision while he loudly cries:
"Oh, joy! our standards flashing from afar!
He comes! he comes! our hero Izdubar!"
He grasps his harp inspired, again to wake
In song-the cry of battle now doth break.

"Nin-a-rad, servant of our great Nin
    Shall lead our hosts to victory!
God of the chase and war, o'er him, oh, shine!
    Tar-u-ma-ni iz-zu sar-ri!

"Let Elam fall! the cause of Accad's woes,
    Revenge of Erech, be the cry!
This land our father's blessed, our king they chose,
    Tar-u-ma-ni iz-zu sar-ri!
Our holy fathers sleep upon this plain,
    We conquer, or we here will die;
For victory, then raise the cry, ye men!
    Tar-u-ma-ni iz-zu sar-ri!"

The minstrel ceases, lifts his hands on high,
And still we hear his joyful waning cry:
Now echoed by yon hosts along the sky,
"He comes! Tar-u-ma-ni iz-zu sar-ri!
Great Accad's hosts arrayed with spears and shields
Are coming! see them flashing o'er the fields!

And he! bright flashing as the god's attire,
Doth lead in burnished gold, our king of fire.
His armor shines through yonder wood and fen,
That tremble 'neath the tread of armèd men.
See! from his jewelled breastplate, helmet, fly
The rays like Samas from the cloudless sky!
How martially he rides his sable steed,
That proudly treads and lifts his noble head,
While eagerly he gallops down the line,
And bears his princely load with porte divine;
And now, along the plains there sounds afar
The piercing bugle-note of Izdubar;
For Erech's walls and turrets are in view,
And high the standards rise of varied hue.
The army halts; the twanging bows are strung;
And from their chariots the chieftains sprung.
The wheeling lines move at each chief's command,
With chariots in front;
                On either hand
Extend the lines of spears and cavalry,
A wingèd storm-cloud waiting for its prey:
And see! while Accad's army ready waits,
The enemy are swarming from the gates.
The charge, from either host, the trumpets sound,
And bristling chariots from each army bound:
A cloud of arrows flies from Accad's bows
That hides the sun, and falls among their foes.
Now roars the thunder of great Accad's cars,

Their brazen chariots as blazing stars
Through Nuk-khu's depths with streams of blazing fire,
Thus fall upon the foe with vengeful ire.
The smoking earth shakes underneath their wheels,
And from each cloud their thunder loudly peals.
Thus Accad on their foes have fiercely hurled
Their solid ranks with Nin-rad's flag unfurled,
The charging lines meet with a fearful sound,
As tempests' waves from rocks in rage rebound;
The foe thus meet the men of Izdubar,
While o'er the field fly the fierce gods of war.

Dark Nin-a-zu her torch holds in her hand.
With her fierce screams directs the gory brand;
And Mam-mit urges her with furious hand,
And coiling dragons poison all the land
With their black folds and pestilential breath,
In fierce delight thus ride the gods of death.

The shouts of Accad mingle with the cries
Of wounded men and fiery steeds, which rise
From all the fields with shrieks of carnage, war,
Till victory crowns the host of Izdubar.
The chariots are covered with the slain,
And crushed beneath lie dead and dying men,
And horses in their harness wounded fall,
With dreadful screams, and wildly view the wall
Of dying warriors piling o'er their heads,
And wonder why each man some fury leads;
And others break across the gory plain
In mad career till they the mountain gain;
And snorting on the hills in wild dismay,
One moment glance below, then fly away;
Away from sounds that prove their masters, fiends,
Away to freedom snuffing purer winds,
Within some cool retreat by mountain streams,
Where peacefully for them, the sun-light gleams.
At last the foe is scattered o'er the plain,
And Accad fiercely slays the flying men;
When Izdubar beholds the victory won
By Accad's grand battalions of the sun,
His bugle-call the awful carnage stays,
Then loud the cry of victory they raise.

COLUMN IV

CORONATION OF IZDUBAR

A crowd of maidens led a glorious van;
With roses laden the fair heralds ran,
With silver-throated music chant the throng,
And sweetly sang the coronation song:
And now we see the gorgeous cavalcade,
Within the walls in Accad's grand parade
They pass, led by the maidens crowned with flowers,
Who strew the path with fragrance;--to the towers
And walls and pillars of each door bright cling
The garlands. Hear the maidens joyful sing!

"Oh, shout the cry! Accadians, joyful sing
For our Deliverer! Oh, crown him King!
Then strew his path with garlands, tulips, rose,
And wave his banners as he onward goes;
Our mighty Nin-rad comes, oh, raise the cry!
We crown Tar-u-ma-ni iz-zu sar-ri!

      Away to Samas' temple grand, away!
        For Accad crowns him, crowns him there!
      He is our chosen Sar this glorious day,
        Oh, send the Khanga through the air!

Then chant the chorus, all ye hosts above!
O daughters, mothers, sing for him we love!
His glory who can sing, who brings us joy?
For hope and gladness all our hearts employ.
He comes, our hope and strength in every war:
We crown him as our king, our Izdubar!

      Away to Samas' temple grand, away!
        For Accad crowns him, crowns him there!
      He is our chosen Sar this glorious day,
        Oh, send the Khanga through the air!

Toward the temple filed the long parade,
The nobles led while Accad's music played;

The harps and timbrels, barsoms, drums and flutes
Unite with trumpets and the silver lutes.
Surrounded by his chieftains rides the Sar
In purple robes upon his brazen car.
Bedecked with garlands, steeds of whitest snow
The chariot draw in state with movement slow,

Each steed led by a *kisib*, nobleman,
A score of beauteous horses linked in span.
The army follows with their nodding plumes,
And burnished armor, trumpets, rolling drums,
And glistening spears enwreathed with fragrant flowers,
While scarfs are waving from the crowded towers.,
And shouts of joy their welcome loud proclaim,
And from each lip resounds their monarch's name.

And now before the holy temple stands
The chariot, in silence cease the bands.
Around an altar stand the waiting priests,
And held by them, the sacrificial beasts.
The hero from his chair descends,
And bowing to the priests, he lowly bends
Before the sacred altar of the Sun,
And prays to Samas, Accad's Holy One.

"O Samas, I invoke thee, throned on high!
  Within the cedars' shadow bright thou art,
Thy footing rests upon immensity;
  All nations eagerly would seek thy heart.
Their eyes have turned toward thee, O our Friend!
  Whose brilliant light illuminates all lands,
Before thy coming all the nations bend,
  Oh, gather every people with thy hands!
For thou, O Samas, knowest boundaries
  Of every kingdom, falsehood dost destroy,
And every evil thought from sorceries
  Of wonders omens, dreams that do annoy,
And evil apparitions, thou dost turn
  To happy issue; malice, dark designs;

And men and countries in thy might o'erturn,
  And sorcery that every soul maligns.
Oh, in thy presence refuge let me find!
  From those who spells invoke against thy King,
Protect one! and my heart within thine, oh, bind!
  Thy breath within mine inmost soul, oh, bring!
That I with thee, O Samas, may rejoice.
  And may the gods who me created, take
Thy hands and lead me, make thy will my choice,
  Direct my breath, my hands, and of me make
They servant, Lord of light of legions vast,
  O Judge, thy glory hath all things surpassed!"

The King then rises, takes the sacred glass,
And holds it in the sun before the mass
Of waiting fuel on the altar piled.

The centring rays--the fuel glowing gild
With a round spot of fire and quickly. spring
Above the altar curling, while they sing!

> "Oh, to the desert places may it fly,
>   This incantation holy!
> O spirit of the heavens, us this day
>   Remember, oh, remember!
> O spirit of the earth, to thee we pray,
>   Remember! Us remember!

> "O God of Fire! a lofty prince doth stand,
>   A warrior, and son of the blue sea,
> Before the God of Fire in thine own land,
>   Before thy holy fires that from us free
> Dread Darkness, where dark Nuk-khu reigns.
>   Our prince, as monarch we proclaim,
> His destiny thy power maintains,
>   Oh, crown his glory with wide fame!

> "With bronze and metal thou dost bless
>   All men, and givest silver, gold.

> The goddess with the hornèd face
>   Did bless us with thee from of old.
> From dross thy fires change gold to purity;
>   Oh, bless our fire-king, round him shine
> With Heaven's vast sublimity!
>   And like the earth with rays divine,
>   As the bright walls of Heaven's shrine."

COLUMN V

ISHTAR AND HER MAIDS IN THE FAVORITE HAUNT OF IZDUBAR

The king while hunting where a forest grows,
Around sweet hyacinths and budding rose,
Where a soft zephyr o'er them gently flows
From the dark *sik-ka-ti* where Kharsak glows;
And Sedu softly dances on the leaves,
And a rich odorous breath from them receives;
Where tulips peep with heliotrope and pink,
With violets upon a gleaming brink
Of silver gliding o'er a water-fall
That sings its purling treasures o'er a wall
Of rugged onyx sparkling to the sea:

A spot where Zir-ri sport oft merrily,
Where Hea's arm outstretched doth form a bay,
Wild, sheltered, where his sea-daughters play;
A jasper rock here peeps above the waves
Of emerald hue; with them its summit laves.

Around, above, this cool enchanting cove
Bend amorous, spicy branches; here the dove
Oft coos its sweetest notes to its own mate,
And fragrance pure, divine, the air doth freight,
To sport with gods no lovelier place is found,
With love alone the mystic woods resound.

Here witching Zi-na-ki oft drag within
The waves unwilling Zi-si; here the din
Of roars of sullen storms is never known
When tempests make the mighty waters groan;
Nor sound of strife is heard, but rippling rills,
Or softest note of love, the breezes fills.

And here the king in blissful dreams oft lies
'Mid pure ambrosial odors, and light flies
The tune in bliss; away from kingly care,
And hollow splendor of the courtly glare;
Away from triumphs, battle-fields afar,
The favorite haunt of huntsman Izdubar.

The Queen of Love the glowing spot surveys,
And sees the monarch where he blissful lays;
And watching till he takes his bow and spear
To chase the wild gazelles now browsing near,
She, ere the king returns, near by arrives
With her two maids; with them for love connives,
joy and seduction thus voluptuous fly
Her Samkhatu, Kharimtu from the sky,
As gently, lightly as a spirit's wing
Oft carries gods to earth while Sedu sing.
Thus, they, with lightest step, expectant stood
Within this lovely spot beneath the wood.

Their snowy limbs they bare, undraped now stand
Upon the rock at Ishtar's soft command.
Like marble forms endued with life they move,
And thrill the air with welcome notes of love.
The *its-tu-ri Same mut-tab-ri* sang
Their sweetest notes, and the *Khar-san-u* rang
With songs of thrushes, turtle-doves and Jays,
And linnets, with the nightingale's sweet lays,

Goldfinches, magpies and the wild hoopoes;
With cries of green-plumed parrots and cuckoos,

Pee-wits and sparrows join the piercing cries
Of gorgeous herons, while now upward flies
The eagle screaming, joyful spreads his wings
Above the forest; and the woodchuck rings
A wild tattoo upon the trees around;
And humming-birds whirr o'er the flowering ground
In flocks, and beat the luscious laden air
With emerald and gold, and scarlet, where
These perfect forms with godly grace divine,
In loveliness upon the rock recline.
Sweet joy is slender formed, with bright black eyes
That sparkle oft and dance with joy's surprise;
Seduction, with her rare voluptuous form,
Enchanteth all till wildest passions warm
The blood and fire the eye beneath her charm;
All hearts in heaven and earth she doth disarm.
The Queen with every perfect charm displayed
Delights the eye, and fills the heart, dismayed
With fear, lest the bright phantom may dissolve
To airy nothingness, till fierce resolve
Fills each who her beholds, while love doth dart
From liquid eyes and captivates the heart.
She is the queen who fills the earth with love
And reigns unrivalled in her realms above.

Beware, ye hearts! beware! who feel the snare
Of Ishtar, lest ye tread upon the air;
When ye her rosy chain of fragrance wear,
When blindness strikes the eye, and deaf the ear
Becomes, and heartstrings only lead you then,
Till ye return to common sense again;
Enthralled mayhap and captive led in chains
Ye then will leisure have to bear your pains;
Or if perchance a joy hath come to thee,
Through all thy joyous life, then happy be!

COLUMN VI

The hour has come when Izdubar will seek
The cool enchantment of the cove, and slake
His thirst with its sweet waters bubbling pure,
Where Love has spread for him her sweetest lure,
The maids expectant listening, watch and wait
His coming; oft in ecstacies they prate
O'er his surprise, and softly sport and splash
The limpid waves around, that glowing flash
Like heaps of snowy pearls flung to the light
By Hea's hands, his Zir-ri to delight.
And now upon the rock each maid reclines,
While Ishtar's form beneath them brightly shines;
Beside the fountain stands the lovely god,
The graceful sovereign of Love's sweet abode.

"He comes; the shrubs of yonder jasmine near
Are rustling, oh, he comes! my Izdubar!"
And thus her love she greets: "Why art thou here?
Thou lovely mortal! king art thou, or seer?
We reck not which, and welcome give to thee;
Wouldst thou here sport with us within the sea?"
And then, as if her loveliness forgot,
She quickly grasped her golden locks and wrought
Them round her form of symmetry with grace
That well became a god, while o'er her face
Of sweetest beauty blushes were o'erspread;
"Thou see-est only Nature's robe," she said.
"'Tis all I wish while sporting with my maids,
And all alone no care have we for jades;
And if with thee we can in truth confide,
We here from all the world may cosey hide."
She hurls a glance toward him, smiling naïve,
Then bounding from the rock, peeps from a wave;
The waters fondling her surround, embrace
Her charms; and now emerging with rare grace,

She turning says:
                "Make haste, my hearts!
Come forth! attend your queen!" and then she parts
The azure waves, to where, in dumb surprise,
The King enchanted stands, and fondly eyes
The Queen divine, while fascinating thrills
Sweep wildly through his breast; as fragrance fills
The rose-tree groves, or gardens of the gods,
Or breezes odorous from the Blest Abodes.

A longing, rising, fills his inmost soul
For this sweet queen who offers him a goal
His stormy life has never known, since he,
His loved one lost beneath the raging sea;
And all his calm resolves to seek no more
A joy which passed and left his heart forlore,
Are breaking, vanishing beneath her charms,
Dissolving as the mists, when sunlight warms
The earth, then scorching drinks the rising dews;
Till he at last no longer can refuse,
And love directs while he the goddess greets:
"Such wondrous beauty here no mortal meets;
But come, thou Zir-ru, with me sweetly rest;
Primroses, gentians, with their charms invest
My mossy couch, with odorous citron-trees
And feathery palms above; and I will please
Thee with a mortal's love thou hast not known;
In pure love mingling let our spirits run,
For earthly joys are sweeter than above,
That rarest gift, the honeyed kiss of love
On earth, is sweeter bliss than gods enjoy;
Their shadowy forms with love cannot employ
Such pleasure as a mortal's sweet caress.
Come, Zi-ru, and thy spirit I will bless;
The Mandrake ripened golden, glows around;
The fruit of Love is fragrant on the ground."

Amid the Dud'im plants he now reclines,
And to his welcome fate himself resigns;

The lovely queen beside him now doth lay,
And leads his soul along the blissful way
That comes to every heart that longs for love,
When purest joy doth bless us from above;
From her soft liquid eyes the love-light speaks,
And her warm hands she lays in his, and wakes
Beneath her touch a thrill of wild desire,
Until his blood now seems like molten fire.
Her eyes half closed begat a passion wild,
With her warm breast, her loves hath beguiled;
She nearer creeps with hot and balmy breath,
And trembling form aglow, and to him saith:
"My lips are burning for a kiss, my love!"
A prize like this, a heart of stone would move,
And he his arms around her fondly placed
Till she reclined upon his breast, embraced,
Their lips in one long thrilling rapture meet.
But hark! what are these strains above so sweet
That float around, above, their love surround?
An-nu-na-ci from forests, mounts around,

And from the streams and lakes, and ocean, trees,
And all that haunt the godly place, to please
The lovers, softly chant and dance around
To cymbals, lyres until the rocks resound,
Of goddess Ishtar chant, and Izdubar,
The Queen of Love wed to the King of War.
And he alarmed starts up and springs away,
And furious cries, to Ishtar's wild dismay:

"What meanest thou, thou wanton brazen thing?
Wouldst thou on me the direst curses bring?"
And lo! the goddess is transformed! the crown
Of her own silver skies shines like the sun,
And o'er her dazzling robes a halo falls;
Her stately form with glory him appals,
For Heaven's dazzling splendor o'er her flows,
With rays celestial; o'er her brow there glows
A single star.

      "Have I embraced a god?"
He horrified now cries; and she doth nod
Assent.
      "But, oh I wilt thou thy queen forgive?
I love thee! stay! oh, stay! my heart you grieve!
He springs beyond the mystic circling ring,
And from their sight thus glides the angry King.
Beneath the wood himself he doth disguise
In tattered garments, on his steed he flies;
And when he comes in sight of Erech's gate,
His beggar's mantle throws aside; in state
Again enrobed, composed his anxious face,
Through Erech's gates he rides with kingly grace;
O'er his adventure thus the King reflects:
"Alas my folly leads, my life directs!
'Tis true, the goddess hath seductive charms,
E'en yet I feel her warm embracing arms.
Enough! her love from me I'll drive away;
Alas! for me, is this unfruitful day!"

TABLET II

COLUMN I

ISHTAR'S MIDNIGHT COURTSHIP IN THE PALACE OF IZDUBAR.

As Samas' car sank in the glowing west,
And Sin the moon-god forth had come full drest
For starry dance across the glistening skies,
The sound of work for man on earth now dies,
And all betake themselves to sweet repose.
The silver light of Sin above bright flows,
And floods the figures on the painted walls,
O'er sculptured lions, softly, lightly falls;
Like grim and silent watch-dogs at the door
They stand; in marble check their leaping roar.
The King within his chamber went his way,
Upon his golden jewelled couch he lay.
The silken scarlet canopy was hung
In graceful drapery and loosely clung

Around his couch, and purple damask cloths
Embroidered with rare skill, preserved from moths
By rich perfumes, to the carved lintel clung
In graceful folds; thus o'er the entrance hung.

Queen Ishtar softly comes, and o'er his dreams
A mystic spell she draws, until it seems
While half awake he lies, that she is yet
Close nestling in his arms, as he had met
Her in the wood, and with her there reclined,
While her soft arms around him were entwined.
Thus while he sleeps she hovers o'er his bed
With throbbing heart, and close inclines her head
Until her lips near touch the sleeping King's,
But daring not to kiss.
                        She love thus brings,
All through his dreams; until one misty night,

While be yet restless tossed, the lovely sprite
Sunk him to deeper sleep with her soft lyre
While hanging o'er his couch consumed with fire
That nestling around her heart-strings fiercely burned
Until at last lulled by the strain he turned
Upon his couch at rest, and she now lay
Beside him closely, when she heard him say:
"My love thou art, but canst not be!" No more
He murmurs, then inflamed she sought the door.
"Perchance the *su-khu-li* sleep not!" she said;
And satisfied, turned where her lover laid;
And to his royal couch she crept again;
Her bliss will have despite of gods and men.
Her hot and burning lips cannot resist
The tempting treasure lying there, nor missed
Shall be the dearest joys of love from her
Who rules all hearts in Heaven, earth, and air.
Her right divine that blessing sweet to take,
She will assert, her burning thirst to slake.

His couch the Heavenly Queen of Love now graces,
And on his breast her glorious head she places;

Embracing him, she softly through her lips
And his, the sweetest earthly nectar sips,
While he in sleep lies murmuring of love,
And she in blissful ecstasy doth move.
Her lips to his, she wildly places there,
Until to him it seems a fond nightmare.

And thus, against his will, she fondly takes
What he her shall deny when he awakes,
The stolen kisses both the lovers thrill:
Unquenched her warm desire would kiss him still,
But his hot blood now warms him in his dream
Which is much more to him than it doth seem;
And clasping her within convulsing arms,
Receives a thrill that all his nerves alarms,
And wakes him from the dreams she had instilled.
"What means this fantasy that hath me filled,
And spirit form that o'er my pillow leans;
I wonder what this fragrant incense means?
Oh, tush! 'tis but an idle, wildering dream,
But how delightful, joyous it did seem!
Her beauteous form it had, its breath perfume;
Do spirit forms such loveliness assume?"

The goddess yet dares not her form reveal,
And quickly she herself doth now conceal

Behind the damask curtains at the door.
When he awoke, sprang to the chamber floor,
As his own maid the queen herself transforms,
Says entering in haste:
                                "What wild alarms
Thee, Sar?" and then demure awaits reply,
In doubt to hear or to his bosom fly.
"My maid art thou? 'Tis well, for I have dreamed
Of spirits, as a Zi-ru fair it seemed."

COLUMN II

THE KING'S SECOND DREAM AND EARLY RIDE UPON SUMIR'S PLAIN, AND HAND-TO-HAND CONFLICT ON THE BANKS OF THE EUPHRATES

The night is fleeing from the light of dawn,
Which dimly falls upon the palace lawn;
The King upon his royal *dum-khi* sleeps,
And to his couch again Queen Ishtar creeps.
In spite his dream to dismal thoughts she turns,
Her victim tosses, now with fever burns:
He wildly starts, and from his *dum-khi* springs,
While loud his voice throughout the palace rings:
"Ho! vassals! haste to me! your King!" he cries,
And stamping fiercely while, his passions rise.
The *sukh-li* and *masari* rush in:
"What trouble, Sar? have foes here come within?
Then searching around they in his chamber rush,
And eagerly aside the curtains push.
The King yet paces on the floor with strides
That show the trouble of his mind, and chides
Them all as laggards; "Soon the sun will rise:
My steed prepared bring hence!" he turning cries.
He mounts and gallops through the swinging gates,
Nor for attendance of his vassals waits.
Nor turns his face toward the *nam-za-khi*,
Who quickly opened for the King to fly
Without the gates; across the plains he rides
Away unmindful where his steed he guides.
The horse's hoofs resound upon the plain
As the lone horseman with bewildered brain,
To leave behind the phantoms of the night,
Rides fiercely through the early morning light,
Beyond the orange orchards, citron groves,
'Mid feathery date-palms he reckless roves.

The fields of yellow grain mid fig-trees flash
Unseen, and prickly pears, pomegranates, dash
In quick succession by, till the white foam
From his steed's mouth and quiv'ring flanks doth come;
Nor heeds the whitened flowing mane, but flies,
While clouds of dust him follow, and arise
Behind him o'er the road like black storm clouds,
While Zu the storm-bird onward fiercely goads
The seven raven spirits of the air,
And Nus-ku opens wide the fiery glare
Of pent-up lightnings for fierce Gibil's hand,
Who hurls them forth at Nergal's stern command,
And Rimmon rides triumphant on the air,
And Ninazu for victims doth prepare,
The King rides from the road into the wild,
Nor thought of danger, his stern features smiled
As the worn steed from a huge lion shied,
Which turning glanced at them and sprang aside;
Now Zi-pis-au-ni fly before the King.
And yellow leopards through the rushes spring.
Upon Euphrates' banks his steed he reins,
And views the rosy wilds of Sumir's plains.

He looked toward the east across the plain
That stretched afar o'er brake and marshy fen,
And clustering trees that marked the Tigris' course;
And now beyond the plain o'er fields and moors,
The mountain range of Zu o'er Susa's land
Is glowing 'neath the touch of Samas' hand;
For his bright face is rising in the east,
And shifting clouds from sea and rising mist,
The robes of purple, violet and gold,

With rosy tints the form of Samas fold.
The tamarisk and scarlet mistletoe,
With green acacias' golden summits glow,
And citron, olives, myrtle, climbing vine,
Arbutus, cypress, plane-tree rise divine;
The emerald verdure, clad with brilliant lines,
With rose-tree forests quaffs the morning dews..
The King delighted bares his troubled brow,
In Samas' golden rays doth holy bow.
But see! a shadow steals along the ground!
And trampling footsteps through the copses sound,
And Izdubar, his hand placed on his sword,
Loud cries:
              "Who cometh o'er mine Erech's sward?"

An armèd warrior before him springs;
The King, dismounted, his bright weapon swings.
"'Tis I, Prince Dib-bara, Lord Izdubar,
And now at last alone we meet in war;
My soldiers you o'erthrew upon the field,
But here to Nuk-khu's son thine arm shall yield!
The monarch eyes the warrior evil-born,
And thus replies to him with bitter scorn:
"And dost thou think that Samas' son shall die
By a vile foe who from my host did fly?
Or canst thou hope that sons of darkness may
The Heaven-born of Light and glory slay?
As well mayst hope to quench the god of fire,
But thou shalt die if death from me desire."
The giant forms a moment fiercely glared,
And carefully advanced with weapons bared,
Which flash in the bright rays like blades of fire,
And now in parry meet with blazing ire.
Each firmly stood and rained their ringing blows,
And caught each stroke upon their blades, till glows
The forest round with sparks of fire that flew
Like blazing meteors from their weapons true;

And towering In their rage they cautious sprung
Upon each, foiled, while the deep Suk-ha rung.
At last the monarch struck a mighty blow,
His foeman's shield of gold, his blade cleft through;
And as the lightning swung again his sword,
And struck the chieftain's blade upon the sward,
A Sedu springs from out the tangled copse,
And at his feet the sword still ringing drops.
The King his sword placed at his foeman's throat
And shouted:
              "Hal-ca to yon waiting boat!
Or I will send thy body down this stream!
Ca is-kab-bu! va kal-bu! whence you came!
The chief disarmed now slunk away surprised,
And o'er the strength of Sar-dan-nu surmised.
The King returns, and rides within the gate
Of Erech, and the council entered late.

COLUMN III

The counsellors assembled round the throne
Within the council halls of *zam-at* stone,
Now greet their monarch, and behold his face
With trouble written on his brow, and trace
Uneasiness within that eagle eye,
While be with stately tread, yet wearily
Ills throne approached; he turned to the *mu-di*,
And swept a glance upon his khas-iz-i.
Uneasy they all eyed his troubled face,
For he had ridden at a furious pace.
The *abuli* had told them on that morn,
How he across the plains had wildly torn

To drive away some vision of the night.
One asked, "Hath our Sardan-nu's dreams been light?
Or hath dread phantoms o'er thy pillow hung?
For trouble on thy countenance hath clung."
The monarch startled at the question eyes
The councillor, and to him thus replies:
"'Tis true, my counsellors and wisest men,
I dreamed a fearful dream Sat mu-si; when
I have disclosed it, if one clear reveals
Its meaning all and naught from me conceals,
On him will I the greatest wealth bestow:
I will ennoble him, and the *sib-zu*
A *ku-bar-ra* for him shall rich prepare;
As my *tur-tan-it* he shall be, and seer,
Decked with a golden chain shall next preside
At every feast, and break his bread beside
The King, and highest rank he shall attain
'Mong counsellors, and mine own favor gain;
And seven wives to him I will allow,
And a grand palace. This as King I vow,
The scribe it shall enroll above my seal
As Erech's Sar's decree beyond repeal.

I dreamed upon my *dum-khi* fast asleep,
The stars from heaven fell from yonder deep
To earth; and one, with fierceful heat my back
Did pierce as molten fire, and left its track
Of flames like some huge ball along my spine;
And then transformed, it turned its face to mine;
As some fierce god it glowed before my sight
Till agony was lost in dread affright.

25

I rooted stood, in terror, for its face
Was horrible; I saw in its feet's place
A lion's claws. It sprang, my strength it broke,
And slew me, gloating over me! Awoke,
I sprang, methought I was a corpse *ka-ra*

Va tat-ka mat sar, talka bit-la sha
Ra-pas-ti sat-ti, ar-id-da! ka-ra,
Va hal-li-ka! lik-ru-bu ki-mi-ta!
The seers in silence stand, perplexed and think;
But from the task at once the wisest shrink.
The King each face soon read:
                    "Ye tell me no?"
And nodding all, concealed from him their woe,
For they beheld within the dream some fate
Impending o'er him born of godly hate,
And durst not to their monarch prate their fears,
For flatterers of kings are all his seers.
The King impatient eyed them all with scorn,
And hid his thoughts by wildest passions born;
And then at last contemptuous to them said,
"So all my seers of trouble are afraid?
Or else in ignorance you turn away;
'Tis well! I sorely need a seer this day."
And they now prostrate fall before his throne,
"Forgive thy seers!" one cries, "O mighty One!
For we this dreadful dream do fear portends
Thy harm! a god some message to thee sends!
We know not what, but fear for thee, our Sar,
And none but one can augur it; afar
He lives, Heabani should before the King
Be brought from *Za-Ga-bri* the *na-bu* bring!"
"'Tis well! Prince Zaidu for the hermit send,
And soon this mystery your Sar will end."
The King distressed now to the temple goes
To lay before the mighty gods his woes;
This prayer recites to drive away bad dreams,
While Samas' holy altar brightly gleams:
"O Samas! may my prayer bring me sweet rest,
And may my Lord his favor grant to me:
Annihilate the things that me invest!

This day, O God! distressed, I cry to thee!
O goddess! be thou gracious unto me,
Receive my prayer, my sins forgive I pray:
My wickedness and will arrayed 'gainst thee.
Oh, pardon me! O God, be kind this day,
My groaning may the seven winds destroy,
Clothe me with deep humility! receive
My prayers, as wingèd birds, oh, may they fly

And fishes carry them, and rivers weave
Them in the waters on to thee, O God!
As creeping things of the vast desert, cry
I unto thee outstretched on Erech's sod;
And from the river's lowest depths I pray;
My heart cause thou to shine like polished gold,
Though food and drink of Nin-a-zu this day
Be mine, while worms and death thy servant fold.
Oh, from thine altar me support, protect,
In low humility I pray, forgive!
Feed me with joy, my dreams with grace direct;
The dream I dreamed, oh favorable give
To me its omen filled with happiness!
May Mak-hir , god of dreams, my couch invest!
With visions of Bit-sag-gal my heart bless,
The temple of the gods, of Nin, with rest
Unbroken, and to Merodach I pray!
The favoring one, to prosper me and mine:
 Oh, may thy entering exalted be!
And thy divinity with glory shine,
And may our city shine with glowing meads,
And all my people praise thy glorious deeds."
Now to Euphrates' banks the Sar and seers
Their footsteps turn to pray into the ears
Of Hea, where, in white, a hand of priests
Drawn in a crescent, Izdubar invests.
Now at the water's edge he leans, his hands

Dips in the waves, and pours upon the sands
The sparkling drops, while all a hymn descant
To Hea, thus the incantation chant:

"O chant our incantation to the waters pure,
    Euphrates' waters flowing to the sea!
Where Hea's holy face shines bright on every shore,
    O Sabit! of Timatu to ye
We pray! may your bright waters glowing shine
As Hea's face, and heaving breast divine!

"O Sabit, to your father Hea take our prayer!
 And may Dao-ki-na, your bright mother, hear!
 With joy, oh shine, as peaceful as the sleeping light,
 O ever may your throbbing waves be bright.
    O spirit of the Heaven, hear!
       Remember us, Remember!
    O spirit of the earth, come near!
       Remember us, Remember!
O hear us, Hea! hear us, dear Dao-ki-na!
Ca-ca-ma u ca-ca-ma u ca-ca-ma!"

COLUMN IV

Before a cave within the Gab-ri wild,
A seer is resting on a rock; exiled
By his own will from all the haunts of men,
Beside a pool, within a rocky glen
He sits; a turban rests upon his brow,
And meets the lengthened beard of whitest snow.
This morn an omen comes before his eyes,
And him disturbs with a wild eagle's cries
That fierce attacks a fox before his cave;
For he of beasts is the most cunning knave;

In wait upon the ground the fox hath lain
To lure the bird, which flying deems him slain.
He fiercely seizes it, as swooping down,
The bird with its sly quarry would have flown;
But the *a-si* quick seized it by the throat,
While the wide wings with frantic fury smote
The beast, and the sharp talons deeply tore
Its foe--both greedy for the other's gore.

And lo! a voice from yonder sky resounds;
Heabani to his feet now quickly bounds,
And bowing, listens to the voice that comes
In gentleness; upon the winds it roams
From yon blue heights like sighing of the trees;
The seer in reverence upon his knees
Now holy bares his head in Samas' rays,
While the soft voice to him thus gently says:
"A messenger, Heabani, soon shall come
With offers rich, to leave thy lonely home.
This eagle sought its food and found a snare,
The messenger will come from Izdubar,
To learn from thee the meaning of his dream
Which goddess Ishtar sent,--a snare for him.
Then to the messenger prove not a snare,
As yonder *a-si* doth the eagle tear."

The seer in fury tore his beard of snow
And cried--
          "Alas! my days shall end in woe
Within these wilds my happiness is mine,
No other joys I seek, my god divine;
I would upon these rocks lie down to die,
Upon my back here sleep eternally."

And Samas urging, to him thus replied:
"Heabani, hast thou not some manly pride?
And thinkest thou no joy thou here wilt lose?
The lovely Sam-kha-tu the seer may choose.
Arrayed in trappings of divinity
And the insignia of royalty,

Heabani then in Erech shall be great,
And live in happiness and royal state;
And Izdubar shall hearken, and incline
His heart in warmest friendship, and recline
With thee upon a couch of luxury,
And seat thee on a throne of royalty,
On his left hand, a crown shall grace thy brow.
Kings of the earth shall to thee subject bow
And kiss thy feet, and Izdubar shall give
Thee wealth, and thou in luxury shalt live.
In silence Erech's men shall bow to thee,
In royal raiment thou shalt happy be."
Heabani listened to the words that came
From Samas, and his brow was lit with shame
To hear the god of war urge him to go
To earthly happiness--mayhap to woe;
But he within his cave now listless turns
When Samas ceased; then to his rock returns,
And seats himself with calmness on his brow;
His thoughts in happy memories now flow,
And he recalls the blissful days of yore
When he as seer lived on Euphrates' shore,
As the queen's bard oft tuned a festive lay,
While soft-eyed maidens dance and cymbals play.

COLUMN V

EXPEDITION OF ZAIDU IN SEARCH OF THE SEER

Prince Zaidu on his steed now hastes away,
Upon the plains he travelled all that day;
Next morn the Za-Gabri he slow ascends,
Along the mountain sides the horseman wends
Beneath the Eri-ni, and cliffs, and sees
The plains and mountains o'er the misty trees
From the wild summit, and old Khar-sak glow
Above them all with its twin crests of snow.
He plunges in the wild to seek the cave;
Three days unceasing sought young Zaidu brave,

And now at last within the glen he rode,
And near approached Heabani's wild abode.
At last he sees the seer before his home,
And with his monster now toward him come,
That walked subdued beside the hermit seer,
Thus they upon the rocks above appear.

"Why art thou here in warrior's array?
The hermit cries. "I know thee not! away!"

"O holy seer, 'tis Zaidu, from our Sar!
The king of Erech, chieftain Izdubar."

"What seekest thou within my mountain lair?"
Heabani angry cried. "What brings thee here?"

"For thee! if true Heabani is thy name;
I seek the hermit seer of wondrous fame.
My king doth offer thee rich gifts of state,
And sent me to thee here to make thee great.
No empty honors do I seek, which void
Of all true happiness, all men have cloyed.
Return then to thy haunts of pleasure, pain,
For thy king's embassy is all in vain."
The seer returns within his lonely cave
And leaves the prince alone the beast to brave.
At last it slinks away within the gloom;
No more from their wild home doth either come,
Three days Prince Zaidu watches the dark lair,
But now his courage turns to blank despair:
The seer hath changed his mind since Samas sought
To urge him forth to leave his lonely lot.
The prince the mountain precipice now climbs,
And peers within while clinging to the limbs
Of stunted oaks, and views the mountain lair;
But all in vain his calls ring on the air.
Then mounting wearily his steed he turns
Away, and unsuccessful thus returns.

COLUMN VI

HEABANI RESOLVES TO RETURN TO ERECH

As Zaidu sadly turns and rides away,
The hermit from his cave comes forth to pray:

"Alas! hath all these wilds their charms here lost?
And is my breast with wild ambition tost?
My lonely cot I look upon with shame;
Again I long to seek the fields of fame,
Where luxury my remaining years
May crown, and happiness may find--or tears;
'Tis true! I should have welcomed the *bar-ru*;
But he hath since returned to Subartu."
His harp he took from its dust-covered case,
And kissed its carved and well-remembered face;
And tuning it, he glanced toward the wood,
And sang his farewell ode to solitude:

    Farewell, ye mountains, woods and trees--
      My heart doth long again for joy;
    I love your wilds and mossy leas,
      But oh, your solitude doth cloy!

    I love to see the *bur-khi-is*
      Sweep stately o'er the mossy rocks;
    And *tsabi* in a wild like this,
      Hear the tattoo of red woodchucks.

    I love the cries of *lig-bar-ri*
      The *nes-i* calling for their prey;
    And leaping of the *na-a-li*,
      That fly in wildest fear away.

    I love the *bu-hir-tser-i* all,
      Khar-sa-a-nu sa-qu-u-tu;

    Hear *cu-uts-tsi* with thunder roll
    Across the skies within my view.

    I love to see the *ca-ca-bi*
      Peep through the pine-trees o'er my home,
    And watch the wild *tu-ra-a-khi*
      And *arme* welcome, to me come.

    Farewell! ye solitudes, farewell!
      I will not moulder rotting lie
    With no one's lips to wish me well;
      O give me immortality!

    But what is fame? A bubble blown
      Upon the breeze, that bursts its shell,
    And all our brightest hopes are flown,
      And leaves our solitude a hell.

The holy minstrel bows his head in woe,
And sweeps the harpstrings with a movement slow;
Then lifts his eyes toward the setting sun,
His evening invocation thus begun:

  O Samas! to the lifting of my hands
    Show favor! unto me thy servant turn!
What man before thy blessèd Light withstands?
    O thou! what mortal thine own words can learn?
And who can rival them inviolate',
    Among the gods no equal thou hast found.
In Heaven who of all the gods is great?
    O thou alone! art great through Heaven's bound!

On earth what man is great? alas! no one,
    For thou alone art great! through earth's vast bounds.
When wide thy awful voice in Heaven resounds,
    The gods fall prostrate to our Holy One;

  When on the earth thy voice afar resounds,
    The genii bow to thee and kiss the dust.
In thee, O Samas! do I put my trust,
    For thy great love and mercy wide abounds!

O my Creator, God, thy watchfulness
    O'er me, oh may it never cease!
  Keep thou the opening of my lips! the fleece
Of purest snow be my soul's daily dress.
Guard thou my hands! O Samas, Lord of Light!
And ever keep my life and heart aright!

TABLET III

COLUMN I

The dark-eyed maids are dancing in the halls
Of Erech's palace: music fills the walls
Of splendor where the Sar-dan-nu enthroned,
His hours is whiling by the maidens zoned;
A whirling garland chanting forth a song,
Accompanied with harps thus sang the throng:

"Heabani's wisdom chant and sing
    To Erech's king our mighty Sar.
When Hea did Heabani bring,
    Who now to Erech comes afar,
He taught him then all hidden things
    Of Ki or bright Samu above,
That to the Mu-di mystery brings.
    Oh, how Heabani we shall love!

Chorus

"Then sing with joy ye Khau-ik-i!
    The Khau-ga chant with waving arms,
The Nin-uit sing Au-un-na-ci
    Give to our Sar your sweetest charms.

"All knowledge that is visible
    Heabani holds it in his glance,
Sees visions inconceivable,
    The Zi his wizard eyes entrance.
Sweet peace he brings from troubled dreams,
    He copies to El-li-tar-du-si,
From a far road by mountain streams;
    Then sing with joy ye Khau-ik-i!

Chorus

"Then sing with joy ye Khau-ik-i!
  The Khau-ga chant with waving arms,
The Nin-uit sing An-un-na-ci!
  Give to our Sar your sweetest charms.

"E'en all that on the tablet rests,
  In Erech's tower, the Su-bu-ri
The beautiful, with glorious crests,
  He wrote for far posterity.
We plead with him to leave us not,
  But Zi-Gab-ri him led away,
When our great Shal-man joy us brought,
  And Elam fled to the blue sea.

Chorus

"Then sing with joy ye Khau-ik-i!
  Il-gi-sa-kis-sat from above,
The Nin-nit sing An-un-na-ci!
  Oh, how Heabani we shall love!"

The maidens note their monarch's moody face,
And turn their songs to him with easy grace,
Of their great ruler tune a joyous lay,
Arid oft into his eyes hurl glances gay;
And trumpets join the chorus, rolling drums,
And wild applause from all the chieftains comes,

Till the grave seers and councillors now cry
In praise of him they love so tenderly:
With arms upraised the mighty chorus join,
Until his heart is filled with joy divine;
And thus they sing with more than royal praise,
Their love for him in every face doth blaze.

COLUMN II

SONGS IN PRAISE OF IZDUBAR AND HEABANI AS SUNG BY THE KHAU-IK-I

Our Izdubar dear Erech raised
  From her distress, when she did mourn;
With joy his glorious name be praised!
  Of a great warrior's daughter born,

And Bel in his own might, him arms,
  To Erech's sons and daughters save;
What other Sar hath glorious charms
  Like his, who saved proud Elam's slave?

Chorus

No rival hath our mighty Sar,
  Thy cymbals strike and raise the cry!
All hail! All hail! great Izdubar!
  His deeds immortal glorify!

Our Izdubar our sons preserves
  To all our fathers day and night,
And Erech's ruler well deserves
  Our highest praise, whose matchless might
Delights the gods! All hail our Sar!
  Whose firmness, wisdom need no praise!
Queen Daunat's son, our Izdubar,
  His glory to the Sami raise!

Chorus

Of a great warrior's daughter born,
  The gods clothe him with matchless might;
His glory greets the coming morn,
  Oh, how in him we all delight!

And thus of Seer Heabani they now chant
His birth and history and hyemal haunt.

Who can compare with thee, O Nin!
  The son of Bel; thy hands didst lay
Upon Ar-ur-u, thine own queen,
  With glory crowned her on that day.

To her thy strength did give, and blessed
  Her with thy love and a dear son;
With Anu's strength within his breast,
  And Ninip sped then to his throne.

When Queen Ar-u-ru hears her lord
  From Erech's city far has gone,
She bows her head upon the sward,
  With pleading hands in woe doth moan.

And to Heabani she gave birth,
  The warrior, great Ninip's son,
Whose fame is spread through all the earth.
  The queen with her own maids alone
Retired within her palace walls
  For purity in Erech's halls.

Like the corn-god his face concealed,
  Of men and countries he possessed,
Great wisdom by the gods revealed:
  As Ner the god, his limbs were dressed.
With wild gazelles he ate his food
  While roaming with them in the night;
For days he wandered in the wood,
  And bu-hir-tser-i him delight.

The Zi-ar-ri Heabani loves,
  That play within the running streams;
With Zi-ti-am-a-ti he roves
  Upon the sands in warm sunbeams.

"The prince returns, O Sar!" the herald said,
And low before the throne he bowed his head;
"Our Zaidu, the bewitcher of all men,
Doth unsuccessful to us come again.
Before the cave the seer confronted him
Three days where Khar-sak's snowy brow doth gleam.
Heabani with his beast in his cave went,
And Zaidu waited, but his courage spent
When he beheld the seer and beast remain
Within the cave, and all his words were vain.
The prince remains without with downcast face
And beg of thee, his Sar, thy sovereign grace."
The king to all the maidens waves his hand,
Then vanishes from sight the choral band.

COLUMN III

ZAIDU'S RETURN, AND HIS INSTRUCTION TO TAKE TWO MAIDS WITH HIM TO ENTICE THE SEER FROM HIS CAVE

Prince Zaidu prostrate bows before the Sar,
Arises, thus narrates to Izdubar:
"Thy sovereign, Zaidu hath his king obeyed,
The royal mission I have thus essayed

As Anu's soldier; I undaunted tried
To urge my mission which the seer denied.
I firmly met the beast that with him came:
Unmanly fear, confess I to my shame,
Came o'er me when I first beheld the beast,
In vain I plead, and in despair I ceased
When he refused, and angry from me passed
Within his cave, where cliffs and rocks are massed;
I climbed, but the wild entrance did not gain,
And for advice have I returned again."

"'Tis well, my son," the Sar to Zaidu said,
"Thy wisdom I commend for thy young head,
Again upon thy mission thou must go.
His might, and strength of purpose, thou dost know,

Before a maiden's charms will flee away;
For he doth love the Zi-Ga-bri that play
Within the mountain gorges. Turn thy face
Again with manly portance; for I'll grace
Thine embassy with two of our sweet maids,
Who oft shall cheer thee through the mountain glades,
Whom thou shalt lead before Heabani's den
With their bright charms exposed within the glen.
Take Sam-kha-tu and sweet Khar-imatu:
They will entice the seer when he shall view
Their charms displayed before his wondering eyes.
With Sam-kha, Joy, the seer you will surprise;
Khar-im-tu will thy plans successful end,
To her seductive glance his pride will bend.
Sweet Sam-kha's charms are known, she is our Joy,
As Ishtar's aid her charms ne'er cloy;
Kharun-tu with her perfect face and form,
The hearts of all our court doth take by storm:
When joys by our sweet Sam-kha are distilled,
Kharun-tu's love o'ercomes us till we yield.
Thus, armed with Love's Seduction and her Joy,
The greatest powers of earth thou dost employ;
No flesh can face them but a heart of stone,
And all the world doth lie before them prone."

Three days Prince Zaidu sat with Kharun-tu
Before the cave within Heabani's view;
Beside the pool they waited for the seer:
From Erech three days' journey brought them here,
But where hath joy, sweet Sam-kha, roving gone?
When they arrived at setting of the sun
She disappeared within with waving arms
With bright locks flowing she displayed her charms.

As some sweet *zir-ru* did young Sam-kha seem,
A thing of beauty of some mystic dream.

COLUMN IV

THE TWO MAIDENS ENTICE THE SEER

Thus in Heabani's cave the maiden went,
And o'er the sleeping seer her form she bent;
O'er him who with gazelles oft eats his food;
O'er him who drinks with *bhu-ri* in the wood;
O'er him who loves the *zir-ri*,--of them dreams,
And sports with them within the mountain streams.
And when the gay enticer saw the seer
Unconscious sleeping with sweet joy so near,
She clasped him to her breast and kissed his brow.
The seer awakes, with wonder eyes her now:
"Thy glory thou hast brought to me!" he saith,
"Sweet Zir-ru comes to me with fragrant breath!"
And with delight he eyes her beauteous form,
His breast warm moved by the enticer's charm.
He springs upon his feet and her pursues:
She laughing flees; to sport with him doth choose.

And now he eyes his hairy body, arms
Compared to Sam-kha's snowy god-like charms,
She give to him her freshness, blooming youth?
She laughing comes again to him,--Forsooth!
Her glorious arms she opens, flees away,
While he doth follow the enticer gay.
He seizes, kisses, takes away her breath,
And she falls to the ground--perhaps in death
He thinks, and o'er her leans where she now lay;
At last she breathes, and springs, and flees away.
But he the sport enjoys, and her pursues;
But glancing back his arms she doth refuse.
And thus three days and four of nights she played;
For of Heabani's love she was afraid.
Her joyous company doth him inspire
For Sam-kha, joy, and love, and wild desire.
He was not satisfied unless her form
Remained before him with her endless charm.

But when his *bhu-ri* of the field the sight
Beheld, the wild gazelles fled in affright.

And now without the cave they came in view
Of Zaidu waiting with sweet Kharim-tu,

And when Heabani saw the rounded form
Of bright Kharim-tu, her voluptuous charm
Drew him to her, and at her feet he sate
With wistful face, resigned to any fate.
Kharim-tu, smiling sweetly, bent her head,
Enticing him the tempter coyly said,
"Heabani, like a famous god thou art,
Why with these creeping things doth sleep thy heart?
Come thou with me to Erech Su-bu-ri
To Anu's temple Elli-tar-du-si,
And Ishtar's city where great Izdubar
Doth reign, the glorious giant king of war;
Whose mighty strength above his chiefs doth tower,
Come see our giant king of matchless power."
Her flashing eyes half languid pierce the seer,
Until his first resolves all disappear.
And rising to his feet his eyes he turned
Toward sweet Joy, whose love for him yet burned;
And eyeing both with beaming face he saith,
"With Sam-kha's love the seer hath pledged his faith;
And I will go to Elli-tar-du-si,
Great Anu's seat and Ishtar's where with thee,
I will behold the giant Izdubar,
Whose fame is known to me as king of war;
And I will meet him there, and test the power
Of him whose fame above all men doth tower.
A *mid-dan-nu* to Erech I will take,
To see if he its mighty strength can break.
In these wild caves its strength has mighty grown;
If he the beast destroys, I will make known
His dream to him--e'en all the seer doth know;
And now with thee to Erech I will go.

COLUMN V

FESTIVAL IN HONOR OF HEABANI, WHO ARRIVES AT ERECH--
INTERPRETATION OF THE DREAM

The sounds of wild rejoicing now arise;
"Heabani comes!" resound the joyful cries,
And through the gates of Erech Suburi
Now file the chieftains, Su-khu-li rubi.
A festival in honor of their guest

The Sar proclaims, and Erech gaily drest,
Her welcome warm extends to the famed seer.
The maidens, Erech's daughters, now appear,
With richest kirtles gaily decked with flowers,
And on his head they rain their rosy showers.
Rejoicing sing, while harps and cymbals play,
And laud him to the skies in their sweet way;
And mingling with their joy, their monarch rode
Before the seer, who stately after strode
Beside his beast, and next the men of fame.
The maids thus chant high honors to his name:

> "A prince we make thee, mighty seer!
> Be filled with joy and royal cheer!
> All hail to Erech's seer!
>
> Whom day and night our Sar hath sought,
> O banish fear! for Hea taught
> The seer, his glory wrought.
>
> He comes! whom Samas loves as gold,
> To Erech grace, our city old;
> All wisdom he doth hold.
>
> Great Hea doth to him unfold
> All that remains to man untold;
> Give him the chain of gold!
>
> He cometh from the Za-Gab-ri
> To our dear Erech Su-bu-ri.
> Heabani glorify!
>
> Thy dream he will reveal, O Sar!
> Its meaning show to Izdubar,
> Victorious king of war."

Within the council halls now lead the seers
With trepidation and with many fears,
To hear the seer explain their monarch's dream.
Beside the royal throne he sits supreme
Among the seers, the Sar, his scribe commands
To read his dream recorded as it stands
In Erech's Gi; who reads it to the seer,
Who answers thus:
                        "In this there doth appear
A god, whose ardent love will lead to deeds
Of hate against thee, Sar; thy present needs
Are great, O king! as fire this love will burn

Until the wicked seven on thee turn;
And blood, alone, will not their fury sate:
The gods will hurl upon thee some dread fate."
In silence, Izdubar the warning heard;
His blood with terror froze, and then was stirred
By passions wild, when he recalled the scene
Of Ishtar's love for him by man unseen;
When she so wildly then proclaimed her love;
And now with hate his utmost soul doth move,
And her bright form to a black dal-khu turned
And furious passions on his features burned.
And then of the first dream he thought, and light
Across his vision broke:
                    "'Tis true! aright
Thy seer hath read! for Ishtar came to me
In the first dream, her face e'en yet I see!
Aye, more! her lips to mine again then fell!
Her arms I felt around me,--breath too well
I know! of fragrance, while perfume arose
Around my dream and fled not at the close;
As frankincense and myrrh it lingered, when
I woke. Ah yes! the queen will come again!"

Then to his counsellor who wondering stood,
Nor heard his murmuring, but saw subdued
His features were, at first, and then, they grand
Became with settled hate; he raised his hand;
"'Tis true!" he said, "Reward oil him bestow!
Then to the waiting feast we all shall go."

COLUMN VI

IZDUBAR SLAYS THE MIDANNU IN THE FESTIVE HALL, AND HEABANI
DECLARES HIM TO BE A GOD

The guests are seated round the festal board;
Heabani takes his seat beside his lord.
The choicest viands of the wealthy plain
Before them placed and fishes of the main,
With wines and cordials, juices rich and rare
The chieftains all enjoy--the royal fare.
This day, with Izdubar they laugh and joke
'Mid courtesies and mirth, and oft provoke
The ringing merry laughter through the halls.
When all are satisfied within the walls,

Their fill have eaten of the royal fare,
With wine they banish from them every care.

The Su-khu-li with tinkling bells proclaim,
"Our Sar would speak! Our king of mighty fame."
Who says: "My chieftains, lords, our seer requests
A test of strength before assembled guests;
Unarmed requires your Sar-dan-nu to slay
The Mid-an-nu which he hath brought to-day.
So stand aside, my friends, behold the test!
Your Sar will satisfy his seer and guest."
The monster now is brought before the king,
Heabani him unchains to let him spring
Upon the giant king. His chieftains stand
In terror looking at their monarch grand,
Who smiling stands, his eyes on the beast fixed;
While they in wildest terror are transfixed.

Heabani claps his hands towards the king,
And the wild beast upon his form doth spring.
The giant grasps its throat in high mid-air,
  And holds it 'neath his arm without a fear.
With sullen choking roars it struggling dies,
While shouts of joy from all the guests arise.
The mighty deed of strength the seer appals,
And at the feet of Izdubar he falls:
"Immortal king! illustrious of men!
Thy glorious strength reveals the gods again
On earth. To thee I bow in reverent fear,
A god returned thou art! O Erech, hear!
Of kingdoms thou art blessed with grandest fame,
That thou among thy kings a god can name."
Again they gathered round the festal board,
And joy and revelry they soon restored.
The revels high are raised o'er sparkling wine;
Through all the night they praise their king divine.

TABLET IV

COLUMN I

THE ANNUAL SALE OF THE MAIDENS OF BABYLON

Hail holy union! wedded love on earth!
The highest bliss which crowns us from our birth,
Our joy! the mainspring of our life and aims,
Our great incentive when sweet love inflames
Our hearts to glorious deeds and ever wreathes
Around our brows, the happy smile that breathes
Sweet fragrance from the home of holy love,
And arms us with a courage from above.

O Woman! Woman! weave thy love around
Thy chosen lover, who in thee hath found
A loveliness and purity so sweet,
That he doth watch for coming of the feet

That brings him happiness and thrill his heart--
For one, of all thy kind who can impart
To him the holiest bliss, the sweetest joy,
That e'er can crown his life so tenderly
He worships thee within a holy fane,
Let not his hope and joy be all in vain!

O thou, sweet Queen! we crown thee in our homes,
And give to thee our love that holy comes
From Heaven to inspire and bless our lives.
For this mankind all hope to take pure wives
To sacredest of all our temples, shrines,
And keep thee pure within sweet love's confines
That we may worship thee, and daily bring
Devotions to our altar,--to thee sing
Our orisons of praise, and sacred keep
Our homes till we shall softly drop asleep

Within the arms we love so tenderly,
And carry with us a sweet memory
Of purity and bliss that blessed our lives,
And children gave from sweetest of pure wives.

Thou art our all! O holy woman, pure
Forever may thy charms on earth endure!
Oh, trample not upon thy husband's love!
For true devotion he doth daily prove.
Oh, shackle not his feet in life's fierce strife,
His weary shoulders burden,--blast his life!
Or palsy those dear hands that work for thee,
And fill his eyes with tears of agony,
Till love shall turn as acid to his teeth,
And thorns shall tear his side with hellish wreath,
And daggers pierce his heart, and ice his soul,
And thou become to him a hated ghoul!

What married woman is untainted, pure?
She, who when married spreads for men no hire,
Bestows caresses on no man but him
Who is her husband; she who doth not trim

Her form to catch the vulgar gaze, nor paints
Herself, or in her husband's absence taunts
Not her sweet purity; exposes not
Her form undraped, whose veil no freeman aught
Has raised; or shows her face to others than
Her slaves; and loves alone her husbandman;
She who has never moistened her pure lips
With liquors that intoxicate; nor sips
With others joys that sacred are alone
To him, her strength; who claims her as his own.

O Beauty, Purity, my theme inspire!
To woman's love of old, my muse aspire!
When her sweet charms were equally bestowed,
And fairest of the sex with hopes imbued
Of capturing men of wealth and lives of ease,
When loveliness at public sale doth please
The nobles of the land to wealth bestow
Upon ill-favored sisters, maids of woe,
Who claimed no beauty, nor had lovely charms;
When crones and hags, and maids with uncouth forms,
Secured a husbandman despite of fate,
And love redeemed them from the arms of hate.

The proclamation Izdubar had made
To bring to the great plaza every maid,

For Beltis' feast and Hergal's now arrives,
When maidens are selected as the wives
Of noblemen or burghers of the towns
And cities of the kingdom; when wealth crowns
The nobles richest, ever as of old,
With beauty they have purchased with their gold.

The festival, the Sabat-tu hath come!
The Sabat-tu of Elul! hear the hum
Of voices filling Erech's streets!
The maids are coming, how each gaily prates!
The day and hour has come for them to stand
And meet the bidders from all Sumir's land;
The day that ends their maidenhood, and brings
Them joy or not. Oh, how the poor young things
With throbbing hearts approach yon gathering throng
To hear their fate pronounced; but is it wrong?
The custom old, Accadia thinks is good,
They all are young and fresh with maidenhood;
The ugly ones as well, shall husbands have,
And their young lives from shame thus they will save.
No agèd maids shall pass from yonder throng
With bitterness,--their heart's unuttered song
For some dear love to end their joyless woe,
And longings unallayed that e'er may flow.

But Love! O where art thou? art thou a thing
That gold may buy? Doth lucre thy bright wing
Unfold to hover over human hearts?
Oh, no! Thy presence to our soul imparts
A sweeter joy than selfishness can give,
Thou givest love that thou mayst love receive;
Nor asking aught of wealth, of rank, or fame.
True love in palace, hovel, is the same
Sweet joy, the holiest of sacred things.
For this we worship Ishtar, for she brings
Us happiness, when we ourselves forget
In the dear arms we love; no coronet
Of power, or countless gold, or rank, or fame,
Or aught that life can give, or tongue can name,
Can reach the heart that loyally doth love,
Nor hopes of heaven, nor fears of hell can move.

Mayhap, this Sabattu, some lover may
All wealth he claims abandon on this day,

For the dear heart that seeming pleads to him,
While her fond glistening eyes shall on him gleam.
A look, a glance; when mingling souls speak love,

Will in his breast undying longings move;
And let us hope that when the youths have lain
Their all before the herald, that no men
Who see their sacrifice will rob their hearts
Of all that gives them joy or bliss imparts;
Or that this day alone will maidens see
Who have not loved, and they will happy be
With him who purchases her as his wife;
Or proud young beauties will enjoy the strife
Of bidders to secure their lovely charms,
And love may bring their husbands to their arms.

The day is sacred, dedicated old
To Love and Strength, when loving arms shall fold
A vigorous husband to a maiden's breast,
Where she may ever stay and safely rest.
The day of Ishtar, Queen of Love! the day
Of Nergal, the strong god, to whom they pray
For strength to bless with vigor Accad's sons.
For many anxious years this day atones.

  This day their Sar the flesh of birds eats not,
Nor food profaned by fire this day, nor aught
Of labor may perform nor *zubat* change,
Nor snowy *ku-bar-ra* anew arrange.
A sacrifice he offers not, nor rides
Upon his chariot this day, nor guides
His realm's affairs, and his Tur-tan-nu rests.
Of soldiers, and of orders, he divests
His mind; and even though disease may fall
Upon him, remedies he may not call.
The temple he shall enter in the night,
And pray that Ishtar's favor may delight
His heart; and lift his voice in holy prayer,

In Nergal's temple rest from every care,
Where he before the holy altar bends
With lifted hands, his soul's petition sends.

Around the square the palms and cedars shine,
And bowers of roses cluster round divine.
Beneath an arch of myrtles, climbing vines,
And canopy,--with wreathing flowers it shines,
There stands a wondrous garland-wreathèd throne,
Where maids are gathered;--each unmarried one.
The timid maids and bold of Babylon
Are each in turn led to the rosy throne;
The crowd of bidders round the herald stand,
The richest and the poorest of the land.

The queen of Accad's maids doth now appear,
We see the burnished chariot coming near,
Ten beauteous bays with proud steps, nodding plumes
Come first; behind, a train of nobles comes;
And now we see the close-drawn canopy
Thrown back by slaves, who step aside, that she
The queen of beauty crowned with lilies, rose,
May here alight. And see! she queenly goes
With dainty steps between the noblemen,
Who stand on either side the queen
Of beauty of the plains, who first this day
Shall reign upon the throne, and lead the way
For all the maids who shall be bought for gold,
And thus the first upon the throne is sold.

She takes her seat beneath the canopy,
Upon the throne high raised, that all may see;
As she her veil of fine spun gold flings back
From her sweet face and o'er her ringlets black,
Her large dark eyes, soft as a wild gazelle's,
Upon the richest nobles dart appeals.
Her bosom throbs 'neath gems and snowy lace,
And robes of broidered satin, velvets, grace
Her beauty with their pearly folds that fall
Around her form.
                    Hark! hear the herald's call!

Behold this pearl! my lords and noblemen,
And who will bid for her as wife, my men?
"Ana-bilti khtirassi ash at ka!"
"Akhadu khtirassi ana sa-sa!"
"U sinu bilti khurassi!" two cried.
"Sal-sutu bilti!" nobles three replied;
And four, and five, and six, till one bid ten,
A vast amount of gold for noblemen:

But see! the bidders in excitement stand
Around a youth who cries with lifted hand
And features pale and stern, who now began
To bid against a wealthy nobleman,
Whose countless herds graze far upon the plain,
His laden ships that ride upon the main
He counts by scores. He turns his evil eyes
And wolfish face upon the youth and cries,
"Khamisserit!" The lover answering says:
"Esra'a!" "U selasa'a!" then brays
The gray-haired lover. "U irbaha!" cries
The youth, and still the nobleman defies;
Who answers cooly, "Khausa'a;" and eyes

The anxious youth, who wildly "Miha!" cries.
"Mine I mine! she is! though you *alapu* " bid!
"A fool thou art!" the noble, leaving, said.
"One hundred talents for a maid!" he sneered,
And in the crowd he growling disappeared.
The measures filled with shining gold are brought,
And thus the loveliest of all is bought.

The next in beauty on the throne is sold,
And thus the beautiful are sold for gold.
The richest thus select the beautiful,
The poor must take alone the dutiful
And homely with a dower which beauty bought,
And ugliness with gold becomes his lot.
The ugliest, unsightly, and deformed,

Is now brought forth; with many wriggles squirmed
She to the throne, where beauty late had sat:
Her ugliness distorted thus; whereat
The herald cries:
                "Who will this woman take
With smallest dowry? She can cook and bake,
And many household duties well perform,
Although she does not claim a beauty's charm.
Who wants a wife?"
                The ugly crone with blinks
Doth hideous look, till every bidder shrinks.
A sorry spectacle, mis-shapen, gross,
She is, and bidders now are at a loss
How much to ask to take the hag to wife.
At last one cries:
                "Five *bilti*, for relief
Of herald I will take, to start the bid!"
"And four of *bilti*, I'll take, with the maid!"
"Three and a half!" one cries with shaking head,
"And she is yours, my man!" the herald said,
And thus she bought a husband and a home.

And so the scare-crows, scraggy ones, now come
In turn; the lean, ill-favored, gawky, bald,
Long-nosed, uncouth, raw-boned, and those with scald
And freckled, frowsy, ricketty and squat,
The stumpy, bandy-leggèd, gaunt, each bought
A man; though ugly as a toad, they sold,
For every man with her received his gold.
The heaped-up gold which beauteous maids had brought
Is thus proportioned to the bidder's lot;
The grisly, blear-eyed, every one is sold,
And husbands purchased for a pile of gold,

And happiness diffused throughout the land;
For when the maid refused her husband's hand
She might return by paying back the gold.
And every maid who thus for wife was sold
Received a bond from him who purchased her,
To wed her as his wife, or else incur

The forfeit of his bond, and thus no maids
In all the land were found as grumbling jades,
Whose fate it was to have no husbandman,
For every woman had a husband then.

COLUMN II

COUNCIL IN THE PALACE

The seers on silver couches round the throne;
The hangings of the carvèd lintel thrown
Aside; the heralds cried: "The Sar! The Sar!
The council opens our King Izdubar!"
The Sar walked o'er the velvets to his throne
Of gold inlaid with gems. A vassal prone
Before the Sar now placed the stool of gold,
Arranged his royal robes with glittering fold
Of laces, fringes rich inwove with pearls,
Embroidered with quaint figures, curious twirls.
Behind the throne a prince of royal blood
Arrayed in courtly splendor, waiting stood,
And gently waved a jewelled fan aloft
Above the Sar's tiara; carpets soft
From Accad's looms the varied tilings bright,
In tasteful order, part conceal from sight.

The glittering pillars stand with gold o'erlaid
In rows throughout the room to the arcade,
Within the entrance from a columned hall.
The ivory-graven panels on the wall
On every side are set in solid gold.
The canopy chased golden pillars hold
Above the throne, and emeralds and gems
Flash from the counsellor's rich diadems.
In silence all await the monarch's sign:
"This council hath been called, the hour is thine
To counsel with thy King upon a plan
Of conquest of our foes, who ride this plain,

Unchecked around; these Suti should be driven
From Sumir's plain. Have ye our wrongs forgiven?

Khumbaba hath enjoyed great Accad's spoils
Too long; with him we end these long turmoils.
What sayest thou, Heabani?--all my seers?
Hath Accad not her chariots and spears?"

Then one among the wisest seers arose
"To save our precious tune which hourly flows,
He should our seer, Rab-sak-i first invite
To lay his plans before the Sar, and light
May break across our vision. I confess
Great obstacles I see, but acquiesce
In any plan you deem may bring success.
The gods, I feel our cause will gladly bless."
Another spoke, and all agree at last
To hear the seer whose wisdom all surpassed.

Heabani modestly arose and said,
And gracefully to all inclined his head:
"O Sar! thy seer will gladly counsel give
To thee, and all our seers; my thanks receive
For thy great confidence in my poor skill
To crush our foes who every country fill.
I with the Sar agree that we should strike
A blow against the rival king, who like
Our Sar, is a great giant king, and lives
Within a mountain castle, whence he grieves
All nations by his tyranny, and reigns
With haughty power from Kharsak to these plains.
I'll lead the way, my Sar, to his wild home;
'Tis twenty *kas-pu* hence, if you will come.
A wall surrounds his castle in a wood,
With brazen gates strong fastened. I have stood
Beneath the lofty pines which dwindle these
To shrubs that grow in parks as ornate trees.
The mighty walls will reach six *gars* in height,
And two in breadth, like Nipur's to the sight.

And when you go, take with you many mules;
With men to bring the spoils, and needed tools
To break the gates, his castle overthrow:
To lose no time, to-morrow we should go.
To Erech, pines and cedars we can bring
With all the wealth of Elam's giant king,
And Erech fill with glorious parks and halls,

Remove these *man-u-bani,* ruined walls.
Take to your hearts, ye seers, poor Erech's wrongs!
Her fall, the bards of Elam sing in songs.
I love dear Erech, may her towers shine!
He seized his harp, thus sung the seer divine:

"O Erech! thy bright plains I love;
Although from thee thy seer did rove,
My heart remained with thee!
The foe destroyed thy beauteous towers,
Sa-mu forgot to rain her showers,
And could I happy be?

Mine eyes beheld thy fallen gates,
Thy blood warm flowing in thy streets,
My heart was broken then.
I raised mine eyes and saw thy Sar
In glory on his steed of war,
And joy returned again!

I saw the foe in wild dismay
Before him flee that glorious day.
With joy I heard the cry
Of victory resound afar,
Saw Elam crushed 'neath Accad's car:
I shouted, Victory!

Away! till birds of prey shall rend
His flesh and haughty Elam bend
Before our mighty Sar!

Beneath his forest of pine-trees
The battle-cry then loudly raise,
We follow Izdubar!

And may the birds of prey surround
Khumbaba stretched upon the ground,
Destroy his body there!
And Izdubar alone be king,
And all his people joyful sing,
With glory crown him here!

All hail! All hail! our giant King,
The *amaranti* for him bring,
To crown him, crown him here,
As King of Accad and Sutu,

And all the land of Subar-tu!
So sayeth Hea's seer!"

The cuunsellors and chieftains wildly cry
Around the throne, "All hail *izzu sar-ri*
Of Su-bar-tu!" and shouting leave the halls
To summon Accad's soldiers from the walls
To hear the war proclaimed against their foes,
And Accad's war-cry from them loud arose.
King Izdubar Heabani warmly prest
Within his arms upon his throbbing breast,
And said, "Let us to the war temple go,
That all the gods their favor may bestow."
The seer replied, "'Tis well! then let us wend
Our way, and at the altar we will bend,--
To Ishtar's temple, where our goddess queen
Doth reign, seek her propitious favor, then
In Samas' holy temple pray for aid
To crush our foe;--with glory on each blade,
Our hands will carry victory in war."
The chiefs, without the temple, join their Sar.

COLUMN III

THE KING WORSHIPS AT THE SHRINE OF ISHTAR

The richest and the poorest here must stay,
Each proud or humble maid must take her way
To Ishtar's temple grand, a lofty shrine,
With youth and beauty seek her aid divine.
Some drive in covered chariots of gold,
With courtly trains come to the temple old.
With ribbons on their brows all take their seats,
The richer maid of nobles, princes, waits
Within grand chambers for the nobler maids;
The rest all sit within the shrine's arcades.
Thus fill the temple with sweet beauties, crones;
The latest maids are the most timid ones.

In rows the maidens sat along the halls
And vestibules, on couches, where the walls
Were carved with mystic signs of Ishtar's feast;
Till at the inner shrine the carvings ceased.
Amid the crowd long silken cords were strung
To mark the paths, and to the pillows clung.
The King through the great crowd now pressed his way

Toward the inner shrine, where he may pray.
The jewelled maidens on the cushioned seats,
Now babbling hailed the King, and each entreats
For sacred service, silver or of gold,
And to him, all, their sweetest charms unfold.
Sonic lovely were, in tears besought and cried,
And many would a blooming bride provide;
While others were deformed and homely, old,
As spinsters still remained, till now grown bold,
They raised their bony arms aloft and bawled.
Some hideous were with harshest voices squalled,

And hags like *dal-khi* from the Under-World,
Their curses deep, growled forth from where they curled.
But these were few and silent soon became,
And hid their ugliness away in shame.
For years some maids had waited day and night,
But beauty hides the ugly ones from sight.

The King astounded, eyed them seated round;
Beneath their gaze his eyes fell to the ground.
"And hath great Accad lost so many sons,
And left so many maids unmarried ones?"
He eyed the image where the goddess stood
Upon a pedestal of cedar wood
O'erlaid with gold and pearls and *uk-ni* stones,
And near it stands the altar with its cones
Of gold adorned with gems and solid pearls,--
And from the golden censer incense curls.
Beside the altar stands a table grand
Of solid metal carved with skilful hand;
Upon it stands a mass of golden ware,
With wines and fruits which pious hands prepare.
The walls are glistening with gold and gems,
The priestesses all wear rich diadems.
The Sar now eyes the maidens, while they gaze;
Thus they expectant wait, while he surveys.
And see! he takes from them a charming girt
With Ishtar's eyes and perfect form, the pearl
Of beauty of them all; turns to the shrine,
When in her lap he drops a golden coin,
And says, "The goddess Ishtar, prosper thee!"
She springs, for she from Ishtar's halls is free,
And kneels and weeps before the monarch's feet,
"O great and mighty Sar I thee entreat,
My will is thine, but all my sisters free:
Behold my sisters here imploring thee!"
The King gazed at the beauteous pleading face,
Which roused within his breast the noble race

Before her heavenly charms transfixed he stood.
Before her heavenly charms transfixed he stood.

"'Tis well! my daughter, I the favor grant!"
And to the priestess said, "Let here be sent
Great coffers filled with gold! for I release
These maids. Let all their weary waiting cease,
The price I'll send by messengers to thee."
And all rejoicing sing a psalmody.
A ring of maidens round the image forms;
With flashing eyes they sing, with waving arms,
A wilderness of snowy arms and feet,
To song and dance the holy measure beat;
A mass of waving ringlets, sparkling eyes.
In wildest transport round each maiden flies,
The measure keeps to sacred psalmody,
With music ravishing,--sweet melody.
The priestess leads for them the holy hymn,
Thus sing they, measure keep with body, limb:

     "Let length of days, long lasting years,
      With sword of power, extend his holy life!
       With years extended full of glory, shine,
      Pre-eminent above all kings in strife.
       Oh, clothe our king, our lord, with strength divine,
     Who with such gifts to gods appears!

     "Let his great empire's limits be,
      Now vast and wide, enlarged, and may he reign
       (Till it shall spread before his eyes complete)
      Supreme above all kings! May he attain
       To silver hairs, old age, and nations greet
     Our sovereign in his royalty!

     "When gifts are ended of Life's days,
      The feasts of the Land of the Silver Sky,
       With bliss, the Blest Abode Refulgent Courts,

     May he enjoy through all eternity,
      Where Light of Happy Fields with joy transports
     And dwell in life eternal, holy there
      In presence of the gods with sacred cheer,
     With Assur's gods walk blessèd ways!"

When they have ended all their joyful song,
They gratefully around their monarch throng;
And kneeling at his feet, they bathe his hands
With tears of joy, and kiss the 'broidered bands

Of his bright robes, then joyous haste away;
And Erech's shame was ended on that day.

And now the Sar as his libation pours
The sparkling sacred wine before the doors
That lead to Ishtar's glorious inner shrine.
He bows before her golden form divine,
Thus prays:
            "In thy fair shrine I bow to thee,
O Light of Heaven! bright thy majesty
As glowing flames upon the world doth dawn,
Bright goddess of the earth, thy fixed abode!
Who dawned upon the earth a glorious god!
With thee prosperity, hath ever gone.
To gild the towers of cities of mankind!
Thou warrior's god, who rideth on the wind!
As a hyena fierce thou sendest war,
And as a lion comes thy raging car.
Each day thou rulest from thy canopy
That spreads above in glory,--shines for thee;
O come, exalted goddess of the Sun!"

 Against the tyrant King I go to war,
Attend mine arms, O Queen! with radiant car
Of battles! ride upon the giant King
With thy bright, fiery chargers! valor bring
To me at rising of the glistening car
Of Samas, send attendants fierce of war!

But goddess Mam-nutu of Fate and Death;
Oh, keep away from me her blasting breath;
Let Samas fix the hour with favor thine,
And o'er mine unknown path, Oh ride divine!
Thy servant strengthen with thy godly power,
That he invincible in war may tower,
Against thy chosen city's greatest foe,
Who brought on Erech all her deepest woe."
And from the inner shrine with curtains hung,
The Oracle of Ishtar sweetly sung:

                "O King of vast unnumbered countries, hear!
                Thine enemy Khum-baba do not fear,
                My hands will waft the winds for thee.
                        Thus I reveal!
                Khum-baba falls! thine enemy!
                        Nor aught conceal.

                "The harvest month propitious shines,
                Array great Accad's battle lines!

55

Before thy feet thy Queen descends,
Before thy will thine Ishtar bends,
    To fight thine enemy,
    To war I go with thee!
My word is spoken, thou hast heard,
For thee, my favor thou hast stirred.
As I am Ishtar of mine Or divine,
Thine enemy shall fall! Be glory thine!

"Before mine Izdubar I go,
And at thy side direct thy blow.
I go with thee, fear not, my King,
For every doubt and fear, I bring
    Relief, to thy heart rest!
    Of Sars, I love thee best!

COLUMN IV

THE KING GOES FROM ISHTAR'S TEMPLE TO THE TEMPLE OF SAMAS

He rose and raised the pendant mystic charms
And kissed them, and the jewels of her arms
And ornaments upon her breast divine,
And then her crown with jewels iridine
He placed upon his brow, and it returned;
And from the shrine in reverence he turned;
To Samas' temple all the chiefs of war
And seers, *pa-te-si*, go with Izdubar.

Before the fire he stands where holy burns
The flames of Samas. In a vase he turns
The crimson wine, to Samas, God, he pours
Libation, and his favor thus implores:

O Samas, why hast thou established, raised
Me in thy heart?--protected? Men have praised
Thee, Holy One! my expedition bless
In thine own will, O God, I acquiesce.
I go, O Samas, on a path afar,
Against Khumbaba I declare this war;
The battle's issue thou alone dost know,
Or if success attends me where I go.
The way is long, O may thy son return
From the vast pine-tree forest, I would earn
For Erech glory and renown! Destroy
Khumbaba and his towers! he doth annoy

All nations, and is evil to thy sight.
To-morrow I will go, O send thy Light
Upon my standards, and dark Nina-zu
Keep thou away, that I may wary view
Mine enemies, and fix for me the hour
When I shall strike and crush Khumbaba's power.

> To all the gods I humbly pray
> To Izdubar propitious be!

> *Assur Samas u Marduk-u,*
> *Ana Sar bel-ni-ya lik-ru-bu*!"

And thus the Oracle with sweetest voice
To him replied, and made his heart rejoice:

> "Fear not, O Izdubar,
> For I am Bel, thy strength in war.
> A heart of strength give I to thee!
> To trust, we can but faithful be!
>   As thou hast shown to me.
> The sixty gods, our strongest ones,
> Will guide thy path where'er it runs;
> The moon-god on thy right shall ride,
> And Samas on thy left shall guide.
> The sixty gods thy will commands
>   To crush Khumbaba's bands.
> In man alone, do not confide,
> Thine eyes turn to the gods,
> Who rule from their abodes,
> And trust in Heaven where powers abide!"

With joyous heart the Sar comes from the shrine
To bathe his brow in Samas' rays divine;
Upon the pyramid he stands and views
The scene below with its bright varied hues.
A peerless pile the temple grandly shone
With marble, gold, and silver in the sun;
In seven stages rose above the walls,
With archways vast and polished pillared halls.
A marble portico surrounds the mass
With sculptured columns, banisters of brass,
And winding stairways round the stages' side,
Grand temples piled on temples upward glide,
A mass of colors like the rainbow hues,
Thus proudly rise from breezy avenues.

The brazen gates lead to the temple's side,
The stairs ascend and up the stages glide.

The basement painted of the darkest blue
Is passed by steps ascending till we view
From them the second stage of orange hue
And crimson third! from thence a glorious view--
A thousand turrets far beneath, is spread
O'er lofty walls, and fields, and grassy mead;
The golden harvests sweep away in sight
And orchards, vineyards, on the left and right;
Euphrates' stream as a broad silver band
Sweeps grandly through the glowing golden land,
Till like a thread of silver still in sight
It meets the Tigris gleaming in the light
That spreads along the glorious bending skies,
The brightest vault of all the emperies.

Now rested from the cushioned seats we rise
And to the stairway turn again our eyes;
The fourth stage plated o'er with beaten gold
We pass, and topaz fifth till we behold
The sixth of azure blue; to seventh glide,
That glows with silvery summit where reside
The gods, within a shrine of silvery sheen
Which brightly glows, and from afar is seen.
Without the temple, burnished silver shines;
Within, pure gold and gems in rare designs.

COLUMN V

EXPEDITION AGAINST KHUMBABA, AND BATTLE IN THE BLACK FOREST

At early dawn the shining ranks are massed,
And Erech echoes with the trumpet's blast;
The chosen men of Erech are in line,
And Ishtar in her car above doth shine.
The blazing standards high with shouts are raised,
As Samas' car above grand Sumir blazed.

The march they sound at Izdubar's command,
And thus they start for King Khumbaba's land;
The gods in bright array above them shine,
By Ishtar led, with Samas, moon-god Sin,
On either sidle with Merodac and Bel,
And Ninip, Nergal, Nusku with his spell,
The sixty gods on chargers of the skies,
And Ishtar's chariot before them flies.

Across Cazina's desert far have come,
The armies now have neared Khumbaba's home;
Beneath grand forests of tall cedar, pine,
And the dark shades near Khar-sak's brow divine.
A brazen gate before them high appeared,
And massive walls which their great foe had reared;
The mighty gates on heavy pivots hung,
They broke, and on their brazen hinges swung
With clanging roars against the solid wall,
And sent through all the wilds a clarion call.
Within his halls Khumbaba is enthroned,
In grand Tul-Khumba's walls by forests zoned
With her bright palaces and templed shrines,
The sanctuaries of the gods, where pines
Sigh on the wafting winds their rich perfumes;
Where Elam's god with sullen thunder dooms
From Kharsak's brow the wailing nation's round,
And Elam's; hosts obey the awful sound.
The giant here his castled city old
Had strengthened, wrung his tributes, silver, gold;
His palace ceiling with pure silver shines,
And on his throne of gold from Magan's mines
In all his pride the conqueror exults,
With wealth has filled his massive iron vaults.
Oft from his marble towers the plains surveys,
And sees his foes' most ancient cities blaze;
While his *pa-te-si* lead his allied hosts,
And o'er his famous victories he boasts.

With Rimsin he allied when Erech fell,
The King of Sarsa, whose great citadel

Was stormed by Nammurabi the great Sar,
Ninrad of Erech, our King Izdubar.
Khumbaba's ally was by him o'erthrown,
And thus appeared to take Khumbaba's throne.
And now within his palace came a sound
That roared through all the forest, shook the ground:
"Our foes! our foes! the gate! hear how it rings!"
And from his throne the giant furious springs:
"Ho! vassals! sound the trump! 'tis Izdubar,
To arms! our foes are on us from afar!"
His weapons seizes, drives his men in fear
Before him with his massive sword and spear,
And as a tempest from his lips he pours
His orders, while his warrior steed he spurs
Along his serried lines of bristling spears;
Among the pines the army disappears.

The men of Accad now in squadrons form,
Arrayed to take Khumbaba's towers by storm;
While Izdubar the forest black surveyed
Of pines and cedars thickly grown, and made
A reconnoitre of his hidden foe.
The road was straight; afar the turrets glow
With Samas' light, and all the gods arrayed,
Ride o'er the pines and flash through their dark shade.
The glorious blaze of Accad's glistening spears
One *kaspu* pass, and now the foe appears;
Beneath the deepest shadows of the pines
Khumbaba stands with solid battle lines
Before the marching host of Izdubar.
The forest echoes with the shouts of war,
As they sweep on with ringing battle cries,
Now loudly echoed from the woods and skies:
"*Kar-ro*! *kar-ra*! we follow Izdubar!"
And through the forests fly the bolts of war.

The foe beheld the gods in wrath above
And Accad's charging lines toward them move,
But bravely stand to meet the onset fierce,
Their mailed armor, shields, no arrows pierce.

And now in direst conflict meet the mass,
And furious still meets ringing bronze and brass,
Khumbaba on his mighty steed of war,
Above the ranks towers high a giant Sar,
And sweeps the men of Accad with his blade,
Till to his breast a heap of corpses made,
And fiercely urged his men to fight, to die;
And Izdubar, with helmet towering high,
His men has led with fury on the foe,
And massacres each man with one fell blow,
Who dares to stand in front with sword or spear,
And fighting by him stands his valiant seer.
The gods now rushing from the gleaming sky,
With blazing weapons carry victory;
The foe no longer stand before the sight,
And shouting fly away in wild affright.
Their monarch turned and slowly rode away;
And Accad's hosts his men pursue and slay,
Until the forest deep resounds with cries.
To save himself each man in terror flies.

COLUMN VI

HAND-TO-HAND CONFLICT OF THE RIVAL GIANTS--DEATH OF KHUMBABA

Now the black forest through, the Sar and seer
Sought for their foe, Khumbaba, far and near;
But he had fled when he beheld the gods
In fury rushing from their bright abodes.
Now from the battle-field the King and seer
The farthest limit of the forest near,
And passing on, the Sar thus to his seer:
"The gods have filled our foeman's heart with fear:
He comes not forth to meet us 'neath his walls."
But lo! within their sight, far from his halls,
Khumbaba stands beside his steed of snow
Held by his queen, and eyes his coming foe.
Heabani cries: "Behold the enemy!
And with his queen from us disdains to fly!"

And Izdubar turned to Heabani, said:
"My seer, methought this King from us had fled;
His army slain or scattered from us fly;
But by our hands this monarch here must die."
Heabani eyed Khumbaba, nor replied
Before the Queen, who wrung her hands and cried;
And Izdubar continued:
                            "He, of war,
It seems, doth lack in skill, and from afar
He scents the battle, while his fighting men
Their raids oft make, and here return again;
His castle we may enter without fear,
And thou his queen mayst have who standeth here,
And now we end the reign of Elam's throne;
So lend thy hand to strike this monarch prone.
My friend, if I mistake thee not, for war
Thou art prepared, since thou upon the car
Wast wont to ride in former years now gone;
And if he falls, a feast day of the Sun
 We will appoint, and may the birds of prey
Surround his carcass on this glorious day:
But stay! this giant I will slay alone,
Although his weight is many *gur-ri* stone;
This giant's form the gods have surely made
An enemy well worthy of my blade."

And Izdubar upon his foe advanced,
Who waiting stood, and at him fiercely glanced,
And naught replied; but raised his glory blade.
Their furious glance, the giant's queen dismayed.

She wildly eyed the rivals towering high,
And breathless stood, then quickly turned to fly,
As Izdubar upon his heavy shield
Received Khumbaba's stroke, and then doth wield
His massive blade as lightning o'er his head,
He strikes the giant's helmet on the mead.
Khumbaba, furious, strikes a mighty blow,
Which staggers Izdubar, who on his foe

Now springs and rains upon him faster blows,
Until his blade with fire continuous glows.
Khumbaba caught his blows on sword and shield
With parries; thrusts returned, and naught would yield;
And thus they fought, the peerless kings of war.
Now Ishtar downward drove his raging car,
And in Khumbaba's eyes her rays she cast,
The giant turned his glance--it was his last;
Unwary caught, his foe has swung his sword,
Khumbaba's gory head rolls o'er the sward.

TABLET V

COLUMN I

CORONATION OF IZDUBAR AS KING OF THE FOUR RACES, AND APPEARANCE OF ISHTAR IN HIS ROYAL PRESENCE, WHO SUES FOR HIS HAND

To Erech's palaces returns the Sar,
Rich laden with Khumbaba's spoils of war.
The land of Ur with grandest glories shines--
And gleams with palaces and towers and shrines.
The plain with temples, cities, walls is filled,
And wide canals, and yellow harvests tilled.
Grand Erech to the sight presents no walls
In ruins laid, but glows with turrets, halls;
With splendor proudly shines across the plain.
And now with joy he meets his courtly train;
Their shouts of welcome rend the gleaming skies,
And happiness beams from his people's eyes.
Within the walls he rides with kingly pride,
And all his chiefs and seers beside him ride;
To his grand palace they now lead the way,
To crown him king of Subartu this day.

Arrayed in splendor on his throne, the Sar
Before him eyes the Kassite spoils of war,

Khumbaba's crown of gold, and blazing gems,
The richest of the Kassite diadems,
The royal sceptre of all Subartu,
Of Larsa, Ur, Kardunia and Sutu
The Sar upon his brow the crown now bound,
Receives the sceptre while his courts resound
With shouts for Sar-dan-nu of Subartu,
The Sar of Kip-rat arba and Sutu,
Of Sumir, Accad, Nipur, Bar-ili,
And Erech, Larsa, Mairu, and Kus-si,
Of Mal-al-nak, Kitu;--the sky resounds--
For Iz-zu-bar-ili, from earth rebounds;
For Nam-mu-rabi, Bar-bels king of fire.
What king to his great glory can aspire?

The Zig-gur-at-u to the skies
His hands have built, where holy fires
To Samas burn; its flame ne'er dies,
To holiness lead man's desires.
He opens wide the fiery gates
Of all the gods at Dintir old,
Ka-ding-ir-a. This day completes
His grandeur--may it far be told
Of our great Sar whose godly gate
Wide opens Heaven's joy for man,
Of Iz-zu-bar-ili the great,
Who rules from Khar-sak to the main.
Within the entrance to the royal rooms,
Queen Ishtar with her train in splendor comes,
Her radiant form with glistening gems ablaze,
And shining crescent with its glorious rays,
Glow with bright Heaven's unremitting flame;
Thus came the Queen of Love of godly fame.
The richest robe of gods her form enshrines,
With every charm of Heaven and earth she shines;

of their wide splendors robs the farthest skies,
That she with love her hero may surprise.
Her train she robes with liveries of Heaven,
To her are all the dazzling splendors given.

The glittering court is filled with chiefs and seers,
When Ishtar at the entrance now appears,
The Ner-kalli, her heralds at the door,
As some grand sovereign from a foreign shore,
The goddess proudly enters with her train,
The spirits of the earth, and tossing main,
From mountains, rivers, woods, and running streams;
And every spirit where the sunlight gleams,

Now fill the courts and palaces and halls,
And thousands glowing bright surround the walls;
Each wafting wind brings I-gi-gi that soar
Above An-un-na-ci from every shore,
And herald Ishtar's presence, Queen of Love,
With music through the halls, around, above.
From lyres and lutes their softest wooings bring,
As Ishtar bows before her lover king.
A halo from the goddess fills the halls,
And shines upon the dazzling jewelled walls.
The Sar and seers in wonder were amazed
At the sweet strains, and glorious light that blazed;
Transfixed in silence stood, as she now spoke,
And sweeter music through the palace woke.
Like fragrant zephyrs, warbling from retreats
Of gardens of the gods, she thus entreats
From Izdubar her welcome, or a glance
Of love; and she the Sar would thus entrance:

"Thy wisdom, Sar, surpasses all mankind,
In thee, O king! no blemish do I find.
The Queen of Heaven favor seeks from thee,
I come with love, and prostrate bend the knee.
My follies past, I hope thou wilt forgive,
Alone I love thee, with thee move and live;
My heart's affections to thee, me have led,

To woo thee to thine Ishtar's marriage bed.
O kiss me, my beloved! I adore
Thee! Hear me! I renounce the godly shore
With all its hollow splendor where as queen
I o'er the heavenly hosts, unrivaled reign
In grandest glory on my shining throne;
And yet for thee my heart here pines alone,
I cannot live without my Izdubar!
My husband's love and simple word shall far
Surpass the godly bond. O let me, king,
Rest on thy breast, and happiness will cling
To all the blissful days which shall be thine.
With glory of the skies, my love shall shine.
O Izdubar, my king! this love below
Is grander here than mortals e'er can know,
For this I leave my throne in yonder skies,
And at the feet of love thy queen now lies.
Oh, let me taste with thee the sweets of love,
And I my love for thee will grandly prove,
And thou shalt ride upon a diamond car,
Lined with pure gold; and jeweled horns of war
Shall stud it round like rays of Samas' fire.
Rich gifts whate'er my lover shall desire,

Thy word shall bring to thee, my Sar-dan-nu!
Lo! all the wealth that gods above can view,
I bring to thee with its exhaustless store.
Oh, come my love! within the halls, where more
Than I have named is found, all, all is thine;
Oh, come with me within our halls divine!
Amid the fragrant odors of the pines,
And all shrubs and flowers, vines,
Euphrates' *zir-ri* there shall sing for thee,
And dance around thy feet with *zi-mu-ri*
And kings and lords and princes I will bring
To bow to thee, beloved, glorious king!
With tribute from the mountains and the plains,
As offerings to thee. Thy flocks shall twins
Bring forth; and herds of fattened, lowing kine
Shall fast increase upon the plains divine.

Thy warrior steeds shall prance with flowing manes,
Resistless with thy chariot on the plain.
Vast spoils, thy beasts of burden far shall bear,
Unrivaled then shall be my king of war;
And victory o'er all, thine eyes shall view,
And loud acclaims shall rend the bright Samu."

COLUMN II

THE KING'S ANSWER AND ISHTAR'S RAGE

Amazed the sovereign sat upon his throne;
And while she wooed, his heart was turned to stone;
In scorn replied:
       "Rise Ishtar, Heaven's high queen,
Though all thy wealth, possessions I had seen
Now piled before me, all in gems and gold,
Of all the wealth of Heaven there heaped of old,
I nakedness and famine would prefer
To all the wealth divine thou canst confer.
What carest thou for earthly royalty?
The cup of poison shall thy lovers see.
Thou sawest me within a haunt away
From men. I lingered on that direful day,
And took thee for a beauteous *zi-re-mu*
Or *zi-ar-i-a* or a *zi-lit-tu*,
And thou didst cause to enter love divine.
As *zi-cur-un-i*, spirit of the wine,
Thou didst deceive me with thine arts refined,

And love escaped upon the passing wind.
Then to my palace come, and me there seek;
Didst place thy mouth upon my lips, and wake
Within my breast a dream of love and fire,
Till I awoke and checked thy wild desire;
Thou earnest with the form of spirits fair,
Didst hover o'er me in my chamber there.
Thy godly fragrance from the skies above,
A sign did carry of the Queen of Love:
I woke, and thou didst vanish, then didst stand

As mine own servant in my palace grand.
Then as a skulking foe, a mystic spell
Didst weave, and scorch me with the fires of hell
While I was wrapped in sleep. Again I woke,
I saw around me *dal-khi*, sulphurous smoke,
Which thou didst send around my royal bed;
And I believed that I was with the dead,
With *dal-khi* gloating over me in hell.
My *su-khu-li* then sought thy presence fell.
Forever may thy wooing cease! for love
Hath fled, may godly praises never move
Upon the lips of holy gods, or men,--
Of thee, the god of Love ne'er speak again!
I loved thee once; with love my heart inflamed
Once sought thee, but my troubles I have blamed
Upon thee, for the dreams which thou didst send.
Go! rest thy heart; and to thy pleasures wend!

For Tammuz of thy youth thy heart once wailed,
For years his weary form thy love assailed;
Allala next, the eagle, lovest, tore
His wings. No longer could he joyful soar
And float above the forest to the sky.
Thou leavest him with fluttering wings to die.
A lusty lion thou didst love, his might
Destroyed, and plucked his claws in fierce delight,
By sevens plucked, nor heard his piteous cry.
A glorious war-steed next thy love didst try,
Who yielded to thee, till his strength was gone:
For seven *kaspu* thou didst ride upon
Him without ceasing, gave no food nor drink,
Till he beneath thee to the earth did sink,
And to his mistress, Sil-i-li, the steed
Returned with broken spirit, drooping head.
Thou lovest Tabulu, the shepherd king,
And from his love continuous didst wring
Sem-uk-ki, till he to appease thy love,
The mighty gods of heaven then sought to move

To pity with his daily offerings.
Beneath thy wand upon the ground he springs,
Transformed to a hyena; then was driven
From his own city--by his dogs was riven.
Next Is-ul-lan-u lov'st, uncouth, and rude,
Thy father's laborer, who subject stood
To thee, and daily scoured thy vessels bright:
His eyes from him were torn, before thy sight.
And chained before thee, there thy lover stood,
With deadly poison placed within his food.
Thou sayst:
   "O Isullanu, stretch thy hand!
The food partake, that doth before thee stand!
Then with thy hand didst offer him the food.
He said: 'What askest thou? It is not good!
I will not eat the poison thus prepared.'
Thy godly wand him from thy presence cleared,
Transformed him to a pillar far away.
And for my love Queen Ishtar comes this day?
As thou hast done with others, would thy love
Return to me, thine actions all doth prove."

The queen in fury from his presence turned,
In speechless rage the palace halls she spurned;
And proudly from the earth swept to the skies;
Her godly train in terror quickly flies.

COLUMN III

ISHTAR COMPLAINS TO ANU, KING OF HEAVEN, WHO CREATES A WINGED BULL TO DESTROY ISHTAR

Before the throne of Arm, Ishtar cries,
And Anatu, the sovereigns of the skies:
"O Sar, this king my beauty doth despise,
My sweetest charms beholds not with his eyes."
And Anu to his daughter thus replied:
"My daughter, thou must crush his vaunting pride,
And he will claim thy beauty and thy charms,
And gladly lie within thy glorious arms."

"I hate him now, O Sar, as I did love!
Against the strength of Anu let him prove
His right divine to rule without our aid,
Before the strength of Ann let him bleed.
Upon this giant Sar so filled with pride,

Let Anu's winged bull in fury ride,
And I will aid the beast to strike him prone,
Till he in death shall breathe his dying groan."
And Ann said: "If thou to it shall join
Thy strength, which all thy noble names define
Thy glories and thy power thus magnified,
Will humble him, who has thy power defied."
And Ishtar thus: "By all my might as queen
Of war and battles, where I proudly reign,
This Sar my hands shall strike upon the plain,
And end his strength and all his boastings vain.
By all the noble names with gods I hold
As queen of war, this giant monarch bold,
Who o'er mine ancient city thinks to reign,
Shall lie for birds of prey upon the plain.
For answering my love for thee with scorn,
Proud monarch! from thy throne thou shalt be torn!"

For Ishtar, Anu from the clouds creates
A shining monster with thick brazen plates
And horns of adamant; and now it flies
Toward the palace, roaring from the skies.

COLUMN IV

THE FIGHT WITH THE WINGED BULL OF ANU

The gods appear above to watch the fight,
And Erech's *masari* rush in affright
To Izdubar, who sits upon his throne,
Before him fall in speechless terror prone.

A louder roar now echoes from the skies,
And Erech's Sar without the palace flies.
He sees the monster light upon the plain,
And calls Heabani with the choicest men
Of Erech's spearsmen armed, who fall in line
Without the gates, led by their Sar divine.

And now the monster rushed on Izdubar,
Who meets it as the god of chase and war.
With whirling sword before the monster's face,
He rains his blows upon its front of brass
And horns, and drives it from him o'er the plain,
And now with spreading wings it comes again,
With maddened fury; fierce its eyeballs glare.

It rides upon the monarch's pointed spear;
The scales the point have turned, and broke the haft.
Then as a pouncing hawk when sailing daft,
In swiftest flight o'er him drops from the skies,
But from the gleaming sword it quickly flies.
Three hundred warriors now nearer drew
To the fierce monster, which toward them flew;
Into their midst the monster furious rushed,
And through their solid ranks resistless pushed
To stay Heabani, onward fought and broke
Two lines and through the third, which met the shock
With ringing swords upon his horns and scales.
At last the seer it reaches, him impales
With its sharp horns: but valiant is the seer--
He grasps its crest and fights without a fear.
The monster from his sword now turns to fly;
Heabani grasps its tail, and turns his eye
Towards his king, while scudding o'er the plain.
So quickly has it rushed and fled amain,
That Izdubar its fury could not meet,
But after it be sprang with nimble feet.

Heabani loosed his grasp and stumbling falls,
And to his king approaching, thus he calls:
"My friend, our strongest men are overthrown:
But see! he comes! such strength was never known.

With all my might I held him, but he fled!
We both it can destroy! Strike at its head!
Like Rimmon now he flies upon the air,
As sceptred Nebo, he his horns doth bear,
That flash with fire along the roaring skies,
  Around the Sar and seer he furious flies.
Heabani grasps the plunging horns, nor breaks
His grasp; in vain the monster plunging shakes
His head, and roaring, upward furious rears.
Heabani's strength the mighty monster fears;
He holds it in his iron grasp, and cries:
"Quick! strike!" Beneath the blows the monster dies;
And Izdubar now turned his furious face
Toward the gods, and on the beast doth place
His foot; he raised his gory sword on high,
And sent his shout defiant to the sky:
"'Tis thus, ye foes divine! the Sar proclaims
His war against your power, and highest names!
Hurl! hurl! your darts of fire, ye vile *kal-bi*!
My challenge hear! ye cravens of the sky!

COLUMN V

The monarch and his seer have cleft the head
From Anu's bull prone lying on the mead.
They now command to bring it from the plain
Within the city where they view the slain.
The heart they brought to Samas' holy shrine,
Before him laid the offering divine.
Without the temple's doors the monster lays,
And Ishtar o'er the towers the bulk surveys;
She spurns the carcass, cursing thus, she cries:
"Woe! woe to Izdubar, who me defies!
My power has overthrown, my champion slain;
Accursèd Sar! most impious of men!"

Heabani heard the cursing of the Queen,
And from the carcass cleft the tail in twain,
Before her laid it; to the goddess said:
"And wherefore comest thou with naught to dread?
Since I with Izdubar have conquered thee,
Thou hearest me! Before thee also see
Thine armored champion's scales! thy beast is dead,"
And Ishtar from his presence furious fled,
And to her maids the goddess loudly calls
Joy and Seduction from the palace halls;
And o'er her champion's death she mourning cries,
And flying with her maids, sped to the skies.

King Izdubar his summons sends afar
To view the monster slain by Erech's Sar.
The young and old the carcass far surround,
And view its mighty bulk upon the ground.
The young men eye its horns with wild delight,
And weigh -them on the public scales in sight
Of Erech. "Thirty *manehs* weighs!" they cry;
"Of purest *zamat* stone, seems to the eye
In substance, with extremities defaced."
Six *gurri* weighed the monster's bulk undressed.
As food for Lugul-turda, their Sar's god,
The beast is severed, placed upon the wood.
Piled high upon the altar o'er the fires.
Then to Euphrates' waters each retires
To cleanse themselves for Erech's grand parade,
As Izdubar by proclamation bade.
Upon their steeds of war with Izdubar
The chiefs and warriors extend afar
With chariots, and waving banners, spears,

And Erech rings with their triumphant cheers.
Before the chariot of their great ar,
Who with his seer rides in his brazen car,
The seers a proclamation loud proclaim
And cheer their Sar and seer; and laud the name
Of their great monarch, chanting thus his praise,
While Erech's band their liveliest marches play:

"If anyone to glory can lay claim
Among all chiefs and warriors of fame,
We Izdubar above them all proclaim
Our Izzu-Ul-bar of undying fame.
> *Sar gabri la isu,*
> *Sar-dannu bu-mas-lu!*

He wears the diadem of Subartu,
From Bar-ili he came to Eridu;
Our giant monarch, who of all *barri*
Can rival him, our Nin-arad *rabî?*
> *Sar-dannu ina mati basi,*
> *Sar bu-mas-la e-mu-ki, nesi.*

Through the grand halls of Erech far resounds
The feast their Sar proclaimed through all the grounds
Of Erech's palaces; where he now meets
His heroes, seers and counsellors, and greets
Them in his crowded festal halls.
Grand banquets far are spread within the walls,
And sparkling rarest wines each freely drank,
And revels ruled the hour till Samas sank,
And shadows sweep across the joyous plain,
And Samas sleeps with Hea 'neath the main.
The jewelled lamps are lit within the halls,
And dazzling glory on the feasters falls.
The rays o'er gems and richest garments shone
Upon the lords and ladies round the throne;
While troops of dancing girls around them move
With , harps and lutes, with songs of love.
Again the board glows with rich food and wines,
Now spread before them till each man reclines
Upon his couch at rest in the far night,
And swimming halls and wines pass from their sight.

COLUMN VI

ISHTAR WEAVES A MYSTIC SPELL OVER THE KING AND SEER, AND VANISHES--
THE SEER ADVISES THE KING TO SEEK THE AID OF THE IMMORTAL SEER WHO
ESCAPES FROM THE FLOOD.

The goddess Ishtar wrapped in darkness waits
Until the goddess Tsil-at-tu the gates
Of sleep has closed upon the darkened plain;
Then lightly to the palace flies the Queen.
O'er the King's couch she weaves an awful dream,
While her bright eyes upon him furious gleam.
Then o'er Heabani's couch a moment stands,
And Heaven's curtains pulls aside with hands
Of mystic power, and he a vision sees--
The gods in council;--vanishing, she flees
Without the palace like a gleam of light,
And wakes the guard around in wild affright.

Next day the seer reveals to Izdubar
How all the gods a council held of war,
And gave to Anu power to punish them
For thus defying Ishtar's godly claim;
And thus the seer gave him his counsel, well
Considered, how to meet their plottings fell:

"To Khasisadra go, who from the flood
Escaped when o'er the earth the waters stood
Above mankind, and covered all the ground;
He at the river's mouth may yet be found.
For his great aid, we now the seer must seek,
For Anu's fury will upon us break.
Immortal lives the seer beside the sea;
Through Hades pass, and soon the seer mayst see."

Thus Izdubar replied, and him embraced:
With thee, Heabani, I my throne have graced;

With thee I go, mine own companion dear,
And on the road each other we may cheer."
"The way is long, my King, and if I live,
With thee I go, but oh, thou must not grieve,
For perils great attend the way, and old
Am I: the suppleness of youth to hold
My strength I need, but it alas! is gone.
My heart is ready, but I fear, my son,
These crippled limbs which Anu's bull hath left
Of my strong vigor have thy seer bereft.

Too weak am I, for that long journey hard
To undertake; my Presence would retard
Thee,--with these wounds; nor strength have I to last
To guard my body in the mountain fast.
But if thou wilt, my strength is thine, my King!
To do thy will my agèd form shall spring
With gladness, and all perils I'll defy;
If need be, for thee will thy servant die."

"Heabani, noble one! my chosen seer!
I love thee, bid thy loyal heart good cheer.
He steeds may take to ride through all the way,
With easy journeys on the road each day;
From perils I will guard thee, and defend;
To-morrow then we on our way will wend."

Equipped for the long journey they appear
Next morn and leave, while Erech's people cheer
Them on their way across the glowing plain,
To perils dire they go--distress and pain.

TABLET VI

COLUMN I

ISHTAR'S DESCENT TO HADES--HER FEARFUL RECEPTION

To Hades' darkened land, whence none return,
Queen Ishtar, Sin's great daughter, now doth turn;
Inclined her ear and listened through the void
That lay beneath of every path devoid,
The home of darkness, of the Under-World,
Where god Ir-kal-la from the heights was hurled.
The land and road from whence is no return,
Where light no entrance hath to that dark bourne;
Where dust to dust returns, devouring clods;
Where light dwells not in Tsil-lat-tus abodes;
Where sable ravens hovering rule the air;
O'er doors and bolts dust reigneth with despair.
Before the gates of gloom the Queen now stands,
And to the keeper Ishtar thus commands:
"O keeper of the waters! open wide
Thy gate, that I through these dark walls may glide;
But if thou open'st not the gate for me,
That I may enter, shattered thou shalt see
The doors and bolts before thee lying prone,
And from the dust shall rise each skeleton,
With fleshless jaws devour all men with thee,
Till death shall triumph o'er mortality."
The keeper to the Princess Ishtar said:
"Withhold thy speech! or Allat's fury dread!
To her I go to bid thee welcome here."
To Allat then the keeper doth appear:
"Thy sister Ishtar the dark waters seeks--
The Queen of Heaven," thus Allat's fury breaks.
"So like an herb uprooted comes this Queen,
To sting me as an asp doth Ishtar mean?
What can her presence bring to me but hate?
Doth Heaven's Queen thus come infuriate?"
And Ishtar thus replies: "The fount I seek,

Where I with Tammuz, my first love, may speak;
And drink its waters, as sweet nectar-wines,
Weep o'er my husband, who in death reclines;
My loss as wife with handmaids I deplore,
O'er my dear Tammuz let my teardrops pour."
And Allat said, "Go! keeper, open wide
The gates to her! she hath me once defied;
Bewitch her as commanded by our laws."
To her thus Hades opened wide its jaws.

"Within, O goddess! Cutha thee receives!
Thus Hades' palace its first greeting gives."
He seized her, and her crown aside was thrown.
"O why, thou keeper, dost thou seize my crown?
"Within, O goddess! Allat thee receives!
'Tis thus to thee our Queen her welcome gives."
Within the next gate he her earrings takes,
And goddess Ishtar now with fury shakes,
"Then why, thou slave, mine earrings take away?"
"Thus entrance, goddess, Allat bids this day."
At the third gate her necklace next he takes,
And now in fear before him Ishtar quakes.
"And wilt thou take from me my gems away?"
"Thus entrance, goddess, Allat bids this day."
And thus he strips the goddess at each gate,
Of ornaments upon her breast and feet
And arms; her bracelets, girdle from her waist,
Her robe next took, and flung the Queen undrest
Within a cell of that dark solitude.
At last, before Queen Ishtar Allat stood,
When she had long remained within the walls
And Allat mocked her till Queen Ishtar falls
Humiliated on the floor in woe;
Then turning wildly, cursed her ancient foe.
Queen Allat furious to her servant cries:
"Go! Naintar! with disease strike blind her eyes!
And strike her side! her breast and head and feet;
With foul disease her strike, within the gate!"

COLUMN II

EFFECT OF ISHTAR'S IMPRISONMENT IN HADES--LOVE DEPARTS FROM THE EARTH--THE EARTH'S SOLEMN DIRGE OF WOE.

When Ishtar, Queen of Love, from Earth had flown,
With her love fled, and left all nature prone;

From Earth all peace with love then fled amain.
In loneliness the bull stalked o'er the plain,
And tossed his drooping crest toward the sky,
In sadness lay upon the green to die;
On the far kine looked weary and bereaved,
And turned toward the gods, and wondering grieved.
The troubled kine then gravely chewed their cud,
And hungerless in the rich pastures stood.
The ass his mate abandoned, fled away,
And loveless wives then cursed the direful day;
And loving husbands kiss their wives no more,
And doves their cooing ceased, and separate soar;
And love then died in. all the breasts of men,
And strife supreme on earth was reveling then.

The sexes of mankind their wars divide,
And women hate all men, and them deride;
And some demented hurl aside their gowns,
And queens their robes discard and jewelled crowns,
And rush upon the streets bereft of shame,
Their forms expose, and all the gods defame.
"Alas! from earth the Queen of Love has gone,
And lovers 'void their haunts with faces wan
And spurn from them the hateful thoughts of love,
For love no longer reigns, all life to move.
An awful thrill now speeds through Hades' doors,
And shakes with horror all the dismal floors;
A wail upon the breeze through space doth fly,
And howling gales sweep madly through the sky;
Through all the universe there speeds a pang
Of travail. Mam-nu-tu appalled doth hang

Upon her blackened pinions in the air
And piteous from her path leads Black Despair,
"The queen in chains in Hades dying lies,
And life with her," they cry, "forever dies!"
Through misty glades and darkened depths of space,
Tornadoes roar her fate to Earth's sweet face;
The direful tidings from far Hades pour
Upon her bosom with their saddest roar;
Like moans of mighty powers in misery,
They bring the tale with awful minstrelsy.
And Earth her mists wrapped round her face in woe,
While icy pangs through all her breast deep flow.
Her bosom sobbing wails a mighty moan,
"Alas! for-ever my sweet queen hath flown!"
With shrieks of hurricane, and ocean's groan,
And sobbing of the winds through heights unknown,
Through mountain gorges sweep her wails of woe,
Through every land and seas, her sorrows flow:

Oh, moan! oh, moan! dear mountains, lakes, and seas!
Oh, weep with me dear plants, and flowers, and trees!
Alas! my beauty fading now will die!
Oh, weep, ye stars, for me in every sky!
Oh, Samas, hide thy face! I am undone!
Oh, weep with me Ur-ru, my precious son.
Let all your notes of joy, my birds, be stilled;
Your mother's heart with dread despair is filled:

Come back, my flowerets, with your fragrant dews;
Come, all my beauties, with your brightest hues;
Come back, my plants and buds and youngling shoots!
Within your mother's bosom hide your roots.
Oh, children, children! Love hath fled away,
Alas! that life I gave should see this day!
Your queen lies dying in her awful woe,
Oh, why should she from us to Hades go?"

Wide Nature felt her woe, and ceased to spring,
And withered buds their vigor lost, and fling
No more their fragrance to the lifeless air;
The fruit-trees died, or barren ceased to bear;

The male plants kiss their female plants no more;
And pollen on the winds no longer soar
To carry their caresses to the seed
Of waiting hearts that unavailing bleed,
Until they fold their petals in despair,
And dying, drop to earth, and wither there.
The growing grain no longer fills its head,
The fairest fields of corn lie blasted, dead.
All Nature mourning dons her sad attire,
And plants and trees with falling leaves expire.
And Samas' light and moon-god's soothing rays
Earth's love no more attracts; recurring days
Are shortened by a blackness deep profound
That rises higher as the days come round.
At last their light flees from the darkened skies,
The last faint gleam now passes, slowly dies.
Upon a blasted world, dread darkness falls,
O'er dying nature, crumbling cities' walls.
Volcanoes' fires are now the only light,
Where pale-faced men collect around in fright;
With fearful cries the lurid air they rend,
To all the gods their wild petitions send.

COLUMN III

PAPSUKUL, THE GOD OF HOPE, AND HERALD OF THE GODS, FLIES FROM THE
EARTH AND INTERCEDES FOR THE RELEASE OF ISHTAR, AND HEA GRANTS
HIS PRAYER

O Hope! thou fleeting pleasure of the mind,
Forever with us stay, our hearts to bind!
We cling to thee till life has fled away;
Our dearest phantom, ever with us stay!
Without thee, we have naught but dread despair,
The worst of all our torments with us here;
Oh, come with thy soft pinions, o'er us shine!
And we will worship thee, a god divine:
The *ignis fatuus* of all our skies
That grandly leads us, vanishes and dies,

And we are left to grope in darkness here,
Without a ray of light our lives to cheer.
Oh, stay! sweet Love's companion, ever stay!
And let us hope with love upon our way!
We reck not if a phantom thou hast been,
And we repent that we have ever seen
Thy light on earth to lead us far astray;
Forever stay! or ever keep away!

When Papsukul beheld in man's abodes
The change that spread o'er blasted, lifeless clods,
And heard earth's wailing through the waning light,
With vegetation passing out of sight,
From the doomed world to Heaven he quickly flies,
While from the earth are rising fearful cries.
To Samas' throne he speeds with flowing tears,
And of the future dark he pours his fears.
To Sin, the moon-god, Pap-su-kul now cries
O'er Ishtar's fate, who in black Hades lies;
O'er Earth's dire end, which with Queen Ishtar dies;
To Hea he appeals with mournful cries:

"O Hea, our Creator, God and King!
Queen Ishtar now is lying prone.
To Earth, our godly queen again, oh, bring!
I trust thy love, O Holy One!
To all the gods who reign o'er us on high
I pray! thus Hope thine aid implores,
Release our queen! To Hades quickly fly!
Thy Pap-su-kul with faith adores.

"The bull hath left the lowing kine bereaved,
  And sulking dies in solitude;
The ass hath fled away, his mates bath grieved,
  And women are no more imbued
With love, and drive their husbands far away,
  And wives enjoy not their caress;
All peace and love have gone from earth this day,
  And love on earth knows not its bliss.

The females die through all the living world,
  Among all beasts, and men, and plants;
All love from them on earth have madly hurled,
  For blissful love no more each pants;
And Samas' light is turned away from Earth,
  And left alone volcanoes' fire;
The land is filled with pestilence and dearth,
  All life on earth will soon expire."

When Hea heard the solemn chant of Hope,
From his high throne he let his sceptre drop,
And cried: "And thus, I rule o'er all mankind!
For this, I gave them life, immortal mind;
To earth's relief, my herald shall quick go,
I hear thy prayer, and song of Ishtar's woe."

"Go! At-su-su-namir, with thy bright head!
With all thy light spring forth! and quickly speed;
Towards the gates of Hades, turn thy face!
And quickly fly for me through yonder space.
Before thy presence may the seven gates
Of Hades open with their gloomy grates;
May Allat's face rejoice before thy sight,
Her rage be soothed, her heart filled with delight;
But conjure her by all the godly names,
And fearless be,--towards the roaring streams
Incline thine ear, and seek the path there spread.
Release Queen Ishtar! raise her godly head!
And sprinkle her with water from the stream;
Her purify! a cup filled to the brim
Place to her lips that she may drink it all.
The herald as a meteor doth fall,
With blazing fire disparts the hanging gloom
Around the gates of that dark world of doom."

COLUMN IV

When Allat saw the flaming herald come,
And his bright light dispelling all her gloom,
She beat her breast; and at him furious foams
In rage, and stamping shakes all Hades' domes,
Thus cursed the herald, At-su-su-namir:
"Away! thou herald! or I'll chain thee here
In my dark vaults, and throw thee for thy food
The city's garbage, which has stagnant stood,
With impure waters for thy daily drink,
And lodge thee in my prison till you sink
From life impaled in yonder dismal room
Of torture; to thy fate so thou hast come?
Thine offspring with starvation I will strike!"

At last obedient doth Allat speak:
"Go, Namtar! and the iron palace strike!
O'er Asherim adorned let the dawn break!
And seat the spirits on their thrones of gold!
Let Ishtar Life's bright waters then behold,
And drink her fill, and bring her then to me;
From her imprisonment, I send her free."
And Namtar then goes through the palace walls,
And flings the light through all the darkened halls,
And places all the spirits on their thrones,
Leads Ishtar to the waters near the cones .
She drinks the sparkling water now with joy,
Which all her form doth cleanse and purify.
And he at the first gate her robe returns,
And leads her through the second; where he turns,

And gives her bracelets back;--thus at each door
Returns to her her girdle, gems; then o'er
Her queenly brow he placed her shining crown.
With all her ornaments that were her own,
She stands with pride before the seventh gate,
And Namtar bows to her in solemn state:

"Thou hast no ransom to our queen here paid
For thy deliverance, yet thou hast said
Thy Tammuz thou didst seek within our walls,
Turn back! and thou wilt find him in these halls.
To bring him back to life the waters pour
Upon him; they thy Tammuz will restore;

With robes thou mayst adorn him and a crown
Of jewels, and thy maid with thee alone
Shall give thee comfort and appease thy grief.
Kharimtu, Samkha come to thy relief!"

Now Ishtar lifts her eyes within a room
Prepared for her, and sees her maidens come,
Before a weird procession wrapped in palls,
That soundless glide within and fills the halls.
Before her now they place a sable bier
Beside the fount-, and Ishtar, drawing near,
Raised the white pall from Tammuz's perfect form.
The clay unconscious, had that mystic charm
Of Beauty sleeping sweetly on his face,--
Of agony or sorrow left no trace:
But, oh! that awful wound of death was there
With its deep mark;--the wound, and not the scar.

When Ishtar's eyes beheld it, all her grief
Broke forth afresh, refusing all relief;
She smote her breast in woe, and moaning cried,
Nor the bright waters to his wound applied:
"O Tammuz! Tammuz! turn thine eyes on me!
Thy queen thou didst adorn, before thee see!
Behold the emeralds and diamond crown
Thou gavest me when I became thine own!
Alas! he answers not; and must I mourn
Forever o'er my love within this bourne?

But, oh! the waters from this glowing stream!
Perhaps those eyes on me with love will beam,
And I shall hear again his song of love.
Oh, quickly let these waters to me prove
Their claim to banish death with magic power!"

Then with her maids, she o'er his form doth pour
The sparkling drops of life-
            "He moves! he lives!
What happiness is this my heart receives?
O come, my Tammuz! to my loving arms!"

And on breast his breathing form she warms;
With wondering eyes he stares upon his queen,
And nestling closed his eyes in bliss again.

COLUMN V

The nectared cup the queen placed to his lips,
And o'er his heaving breast the nectar drips,
And now his arms are folded round his queen,
And her fond kisses he returns again;
And see! they bring to him his harp of gold,
And from its strings, sweet music as of old
His skilful hands wake through the sounding domes;
Oh, how his Song of Love wakes those dark rooms!

"My Queen of Love comes to my arms!
  Her faithful eyes have sought for me,
My Love comes to me with her charms;
  Let all the world now happy be!
    My queen has come again!

Forever, dearest, let me rest
  Upon the bosom of my queen!
Thy lips of love are honeyed best;
  Come! let us fly to bowering green!
    To our sweet bower again.

O Love on Earth! O Love in Heaven!
  That dearest gift which gods have given,
Through all my soul let it be driven,
  And make my heart its dearest haven,
    For Love returns the kiss!

Oh! let me pillow there within
  Thy breast, and, oh, so sweetly rest,
My life anew shall there begin;
  On thy sweet charms, oh, let me feast!
    Life knows no sweeter bliss.

Oh, let me feast upon thy lips,
  As honey-bird the nectar sips,
And drink new rapture through my lips,
  As honey-bee its head thus drips
    In nectarine abyss!

O Love, sweet queen I my heart is thine!
  My Life I clasp within mine arms!
My fondest charmer, queen divine!
  My soul surrenders to thy charms,
    In bliss would fly away.

No dearer joy than this I want;
  If love is banished from that life
There bodyless, my soul would pant,
  And pine away in hopeless grief,
      If love be fled away.

If Love should bide and fold her wings
  In bowers of yonder gleaming skies,
Unmeaning then each bard oft sings
  Of bliss that lives on earth and dies,--
      I want such love as this.

I want thy form, thy loving breast,
  Mine arms of love surrounding thee,
And on thy bosom sweetly rest,
  Or else that world were dead to me.
      No other life is bliss.

If it is thus, my queen, I go
  With joy to yonder blissful clime;
But if not so, then let me flow
  To soil and streams through changing time,
      To me would be more bliss.

For then, in blooming flowerets, I
  Could earth adorn, my soul delight,
And never thus on earth could die;
  For though I should be hid from sight,
      Would spring again with joy!

And sing as some sweet warbling bird,
  Or in the breezes wave as grain,
As yellow sun-birds there have whirred
  On earth, could I thus live again,
      That beauteous world enjoy!

'Mid safflower-fields or waving cane,
  Or in the honeysuckles lie,
In forms of life would breathe again,
  Enjoy Earth's sweetest revelry,
      And ever spring again!

Each life to me new joys would bring,
  In breast of beast or bird or flower,
In each new form new joys would spring,
  And happy, ever, Love would soar!
      Triumphant filled with joy!

In jujube or tamarisk
　　Perhaps would come to life again,
Or in the form of fawns would frisk
　　'Mid violets upon the plain;
　　　　But I should live again!

And throb beneath the glistening dew,
　　In bamboo tufts, or mango-trees,
In lotus bloom, and spring anew,
　　In rose-tree bud, or such as these
　　　　On Earth return again!

And I should learn to love my mate,
　　In beast or singing bird or flower,
For kiss of love in hope could wait;
　　Perhaps I then would come that hour,
　　　　In form I have again!

And love you say, my queen, is there-,
　　Where I can breathe with life anew?
But is it so? My Love, beware!
　　For some things oft are false, some true,
　　　　But I thee trust again!

We fly away! from gates away!
　　Oh, life of bliss! Oh, breath of balm!
With wings we tread the Silver Way,
　　To trailing vines and feathery palm,
　　　　To bower of love again."

COLUMN VI

**ESCAPE OF TAMMUZ FROM HADES--HIS DEATH IN THE CLOUDS-FUNERAL
PROCESSION OF THE GODS-ISHTAR'S ELEGY OVER THE DEATH OF TAMMUZ--
HIS REVIVAL IN HADES, WHERE HE IS CROWNED AS THE LORD OF HADES--
ISHTAR'S RETURN BRINGS LIGHT AND LOVE BACK TO EARTH.**

But see! they pass from those dark gates and walls,
And fly upon the breeze from Hades' halls,
Hark! hark! the sounding harp is stilled! it falls
From Tammuz's hands! Oh, how its wailing calls
To you bright *zi-ni* flying through the skies,
See! one sweet spirit of the wind swift flies
And grasps the wailing harp before it ends
Its wail of woe, and now beneath it bends,

With silent pinions listening to its strings,
Wild sobbing on the winds;--with wailing rings
The conscious harp, and trembles in her hands.

A rush of pinions comes from myriad lands,
With moanings sends afar the awful tale,
And mourners brings with every whispering gale.
And see! the queen's companion fainting sinks!
She lays him on that cloud with fleecy brinks!
And oh! his life is ebbing fast away!
She wildly falls upon his breast, and gray
Her face becomes with bitter agony.
She tearless kneels, wrapt in her misery
And now upon his breast she lays her head,
With tears that gods, alas! with men must shed;
She turning, sobs to her sweet waiting maids,
Who weeping o'er her stand with bended heads:
"Assemble, oh, my maids, in mourning here,
The gods! and spirits of the earth bring near!"

They come! they come! three hundred spirits high,
The heavenly spirits come! the I-gi-gi!
From Heaven's streams and mouths and plains and vales,
And gods by thousands on the wings of gales.
The spirits of the earth, An-un-na-ci,
Now join around their sisters of the sky.
Hark! hear her weeping to the heavenly throng,
Imploring them to chant their mournful song:

"With your gold lyres, the dirge, oh, sing with me!
And moan with me, with your sweet melody;
With swelling notes, as zephyrs softly wail,
And cry with me as sobbing of the gale.
O Earth! dear Earth! oh, wail with thy dead trees!
With sounds of mountain torrents, moaning seas!
And spirits of the lakes, and streams, and vales,
And Zi-ku-ri of mountains' track-less trail,
join our bright legions with your queen! Oh, weep
With your sad tears, dear spirits of the deep!
Let all the mournful sounds of earth be heard,
The breeze hath carried stored from beast and bird;
Join the sweet notes of doves for their lost love
To the wild moans of hours,--wailing move;

Let choirs of Heaven and of the earth then peal,
All living beings my dread sorrow feel!
Oh, come with saddest, weirdest melody,
join earth and sky in one sweet threnody!"

Ten thousand times ten thousand now in line,
In all the panoplies of gods divine;
A million crowns are shining in the light,
A million sceptres, robes of purest white!
Ten thousand harps and lutes and golden lyres
Are waiting now to start the Heavenly choirs.

And lo! a chariot from Heaven comes,
While halves rise from yonder sapphire domes;
A chariot incrusted with bright gems,
A blaze of glory shines from diadems.
See! in the car the queen o'er Tammuz bends,
And nearer the procession slowly wends,
Her regal diadem with tears is dimmed;
And her bright form by sorrow is redeemed
To sweeter, holier beauty in her woe;
Her tears a halo form and brighter flow.

Caparisoned with pearls, ten milk-white steeds
Are harnessed to her chariot that leads;
On snow-white swans beside her ride her maids,
They come! through yonder silver cloudy glades!
Behind her chariot ten sovereigns ride;
Behind them comes all Heaven's lofty pride,
On pale white steeds, the chargers of the skies.
The clouds of snowy pinions rustling rise!
But hark! what is that strain of melody
That fills our souls with grandest euphony?
Hear how it swells and dies upon the breeze!
To softest whisper of the leaves of trees;
Then sweeter, grander, nobler, sweeping comes,
Like myriad lyres that peal through Heaven's domes.
But, oh! how sad and sweet the notes now come!
Like music of the spheres that softly hum;
It rises, falls, with measured melody,

With saddest notes and mournful symphony.
From all the universe sad notes repeat
With doleful strains of woe transcendent, sweet;
Hush! hear the song! my throbbing heart be still!
The songs of gods above the heavens fill!

     "Oh, weep with your sweet tears, and mourning chant,
       O'er this dread loss of Heaven's queen.
     With her, O sisters, join your sweetest plaint
       O'er our dear Tammuz, Tammuz slain.
     Come, all ye spirits, with your drooping wings,
       No more to us sweet joy he brings;
          Ah, me, my brother!

Oh, weep! oh, weep! ye spirits of the air,
  Oh, weep! oh, weep! An-un-na-ci!
Our own dear queen is filled with dread despair.
  Oh, pour your tears, dear earth and sky,
Oh, weep with bitter tears, O dear Sedu,
O'er fearful deeds of Nin-azu;
          Ah, me, my brother!

Let joy be stilled! and every hope be dead!
  And tears alone our hearts distil.
My love has gone!--to darkness he has fled;
  Dread sorrow's cup for us, oh, fill!
And weep for Tammuz we have held so dear,
Sweet sisters of the earth and air;
          Ah, me, my sister!

Oh, come ye, dearest, dearest Zi-re-nu,
  With grace and mercy help us bear
Our loss and hers; our weeping queen, oh, see!
  And drop with us a sister's tear.
Before your eyes our brother slain! oh, view;
Oh, weep with us o'er him so true;
          Ah, me, his sister!

 The sky is dead; its beauty all is gone,
  Oh, weep, ye clouds, for my dead love!
Your queen in her dread sorrow now is prone.
  O rocks and hills in tears, oh, move!
And all my heavenly flowerets for me weep,
O'er him who now in death doth sleep;
          Ah, me, my Tammuz!

Oh, drop o'er him your fragrant dewy tears,
  For your own queen who brings you joy,
For Love, the Queen of Love, no longer cheers,
  Upon my heart it all doth cloy.
Alas! I give you love, nor can receive,
O all my children for me grieve;
          Ah, me, my Tammuz!

Alas! alas! my heart is dying--dead!
  With all these bitter pangs of grief
Despair hath fallen on my queenly head,
  Oh, is there, sisters, no relief?
Hath Tammuz from me ever, ever, gone?
My heart is dead, and turned to stone;
          Ah, me, his queen!

My sister spirits, O my brothers dear,
  My sorrow strikes me to the earth;
Oh, let me die! I now no fate can fear,
  My heart is left a fearful dearth.
Alas, from me all joy! all joy! hath gone;
Oh, Ninazu, what hast thou done?
     Ah, me, his queen!"

To Hades' world beyond our sight they go,
And leave upon the skies Mar-gid-da's glow,
That shines eternally along the sky,
The road where souls redeemed shall ever fly.
Prince Tammuz now again to life restored,
Is crowned in Hades as its King and Lord,

And Ishtar's sorrow thus appeased, she flies
To earth, and fills with light and love the skies.

TABLET VII

COLUMN I

THE KING AND SEER CONVERSING ON THEIR WAY TO KHASISADRA-- INTERPRETATION OF THE KING'S DREAM IN THE PALACE ON THE NIGHT OF THE FESTIVAL

"The dream, my seer, which I beheld last night
Within our tent, may bring to us delight.
I saw a mountain summit flash with fire,
That like a royal robe or god's attire
Illumined all its sides. The omen might
Some joy us bring, for it was shining bright."
And thus the Sar revealed to him his dream.

Heabani said, "My friend, though it did seem
Propitious, yet, deceptive was it all,
And came in memory of Elam's fall.
The mountain burning was Khumbaba's halls
We fired, when all his soldiers from the walls
Had fled;--the *ni-takh-garri*, --on that morn,
Of such deceptive dreams, I would thee warn!"

Some twenty *kaspu* they have passed this day,
At thirty *kaspu* they dismount to pray
And raise an altar, Samas to beseech
That they their journey's end may safely reach.
The tent now raised, their evening meal prepare
Beneath the forest in the open air;
And Izdubar brought from the tent the dream
He dreamed the festal night when Ishtar came
To him;--he reads it from a written scroll:
"Upon my sight a vision thus did fall:
I saw two men that night beside a god;
One man a turban wore, and fearless trod.
The god reached forth his hand and struck him down
Like mountains hurled on fields of corn, thus prone

He lay; and Izdubar then saw the god
Was Anatu, who struck him to the sod.
The troubler of all men, Samu's fierce queen,
Thus struck the turbaned man upon the plain.
He ceased his struggling, to his friend thus said:
'My friend, thou askest not why I am laid
Here naked, nor my low condition heed.
Accursèd thus I lie upon the mead;
The god has crushed me, burned my limbs with fire.'

The vision from mine eyes did then expire.
A third dream came to me, which I yet fear,
The first beyond my sight doth disappear.
A fire-god thundering o'er the earth doth ride;
The door of darkness burning flew aside;
Like a fierce stream of lightning, blazing fire,
Beside me roared the god with fury dire,
And hurled wide death on earth on every side;
And quickly from my sight it thus did glide,
And in its track I saw a palm-tree green
Upon a waste, naught else by me was seen."

Heabani pondering, thus explained the dream:
"My friend, the god was Samas, who doth gleam
With his bright glory, power, our God and Lord,
Our great Creator King, whose thunders roared
By thee, as through yon sky he takes his way;
For his great favor we should ever pray.
The man thou sawest lying on the plain
Was thee, O King,--to fight such power is vain.
Thus Anatu will strike thee with disease,
Unless thou soon her anger shalt appease;
And if thou warrest with such foes divine,
The fires of death shall o'er thy kingdom shine.
The palm-tree green upon the desert left
Doth show that we of hope are not bereft;
The gods for us their shares have surely weft,
One shall be taken, and the other left."

COLUMN II

CONTEST WITH THE DRAGONS IN THE MOUNTAINS--THE SEER IS MORTALLY WOUNDED--HIS CALM VIEW OF THE HEREAFTER

"O Mam-mitu, thou god of fate and death!
Thou spirit of fierce hate and parting breath,

Thou banisher of joy! O ghastly Law,
That gathers countless forces in thy maw!
A phantom! curse! and oft a blessing, joy!
All Heaven and earth thy hands shall e'er employ.
With blessings come, or curses to us bring,
The god who fails not with her hovering wing;
Nor god, nor man thy coming e'er may ken,
O mystery! thy ways none can explain."

If thou must come in earthquakes, fire, and flood,
Or pestilence and eftsoons cry for blood,
Thou comest oft with voice of sweetest love,
Our dearest, fondest passions, hopes, to move;
And men have worshipped thee in every form,
In fear have praised thee, sought thy feet to charm.
We reek not if you blessings, curses bring,
For men oft change thy noiseless, ghoulish wing.
And yet, thou comest, goddess Mam-mitu,
To bring with thee the feet of Nin-a-zu,
Two sister ghouls, remorseless, tearless, wan,
We fear ye not; ye *bu'i-du*, begone!

Sweet life renews itself in holy love,
Your victory is naught! Ye vainly rove
Across our pathway with yours forms inane,
For somewhere, though we die, we live again.
  The soul departed shall in glory shine,
As burnished gold its form shall glow divine,
And Samas there shall grant to us new life;
And Merodac, the eldest son, all strife

Shall end in peace in yonder Blest Abode,
Where happiness doth crown our glorious God.

  The sacred waters there shall ever flow,
To Anat's arms shall all the righteous go;
The queen of Anu, Heaven's king, our hands
Outstretched will clasp, and through the glorious lands
Will lead us to the place of sweet delights;
The land that glows on yonder blessèd heights
Where milk and honey from bright fountains flow.
And nectar to our lips, all sorrows, woe,
Shall end in happiness beside the Stream
Of Life, and joy for us shall ever gleam;
Our hearts with thankfulness shall sweetly sing
And grander blissfulness each day will bring.

And if we do not reach that spirit realm,
Where bodyless each soul may ages whelm

With joy unutterable; still we live,
With bodies knew upon dear Earth, and give
Our newer life to children with our blood.
Or if these blessings we should miss; in wood,
Or glen, or garden, field, or emerald seas,
Our forms shall spring again; in such as these
We see around us throbbing with sweet life,
In trees or flowerets.
                    This needs no belief
On which to base the fabric of a dream,
For Earth her children from death doth redeem,
And each contributes to continuous bloom;
So go your way! ye sisters, to your gloom!

Far on their road have come the king of fame
And seer, within the land of Mas they came,
Nor knew that Fate was hovering o'er their way,
In gentle converse they have passed the day.
Some twenty *kaspu* o'er the hills and plain,
They a wild forest in the mountain gain,

In a deep gorge they rode through thickets wild,
Beneath the pines; now to a pass they filed,
And lo! two dragons near a cave contend
Their path! with backs upreared their coils unbend,
Extend their ravenous jaws with a loud roar
That harshly comes from mouths of clotted gore.

The sky o'erhead with lowering clouds is cast,
Which Anu in his rage above them massed.
Dark tempests fly above from Rimmon's breath,
Who hovers o'er them with the gods of death;
The wicked seven winds howl wildly round,
And crashing cedars falling shake the ground.
Now Tsil-lattu her black wings spreads o'er all,
Dark shrouding all the forest with her pall,
And from his steed for safety each dismounts,
And o'er their heads now break the ebon founts.
But hark! what is that dreadful roaring noise?
The dragons come! Their flaming crests they poise
Above, and nearer blaze their eyes of fire,
And see! upon them rush the monsters dire.

The largest springs upon the giant Sar,
Who parrying with the sword he used in war,
With many wounds it pierces, drives it back;
Again it comes, renews its fierce attack,
With fangs outspread its victims to devour,

High o'er the monarch's head its crest doth tower,
Its fiery breath upon his helm doth glow.

Exposed its breast! he strikes! his blade drives through
Its vitals! Dying now it shakes the ground,
And furious lashes all the forest round.
But hark! what is that awful lingering shriek
And cries of woe, that on his ears wild break?
A blinding flash, see! all the land reveals,
With dreadful roars, and darkness quick conceals
The fearful sight, to ever after come

Before his eyes, wherever he may roam.
The King, alas! too late Heabani drags
From the beast's fangs, that dies beneath the crags
O'erhanging near the cave. And now a din
Loud comes from *dalkhi* that around them spin
In fierce delight, while hellish voices rise
In harsh and awful mockery; the cries
Of agony return with taunting groans,
And mock with their fell hate those piteous moans.

Amazed stands Izdubar above his seer,
Nor hears the screams, nor the fierce *dalkhi's* jeer;
Beneath the flashing lightnings he soon found
The cave, and lays the seer upon the ground.
His breaking heart now cries in agony,
"Heabani! O my seer, thou must not die!
Alas! dread Mam-mitu hath led us here,
Awake for me! arouse! my noble seer!
I would to gods of Erech I had died
For thee! my seer! my strength! my kingdom's pride!"

The seer at last revives and turns his face
With love that death touched not, his hand doth place
With friendly clasp in that of his dear king,
And says:
          "Grieve not, belovèd friend, this thing
Called death at last must come, why should we fear?
'Tis Hades' mist that opens for thy seer!
The gods us brought, nor asked consent, and life
They give and take away from all this strife
That must be here, my life I end on earth;
Both joy and sorrow I have seen from birth;
To Hades' awful land, whence none return,
Heabani's face in sorrow now must turn.
My love for thee, mine only pang reveals,
For this alone I grieve."
                    A teardrop steals

Across his features, shining 'neath the light
The King has lit to make the cavern bright.

"But oh, friend Izdubar, my King, when I
From this dear earth to waiting Hades fly,
Grieve not; and when to Erech you return,
Thou shalt in glory reign, and Zaidu learn
As thy companion all that thine own heart
Desires, thy throne thou wilt to him impart.
The female, Samkha, whom he brought to me
Is false, in league with thine own enemy.
And she will cause thee mischief, seek to drive
Thee from thy throne; but do not let her live
Within the walls of Erech, for the gods
Have not been worshipped in their high abodes.
When thou returnest, to the temple go,
And pray the gods to turn from thee the blow
Of Anu's fury, the strong god, who reigns
Above, and sent these woes upon the plains.
His anger raised against thee, even thee,
Must be allayed, or thy goods thou shalt see,
And kingdom, all destroyed by his dread power.
But Khasisadra will to thee give more
Advice when thou shalt meet the ancient seer,
For from thy side must I soon disappear."
The seer now ceased, and on his couch asleep
Spoke not, and Izdubar alone doth weep.

And thus twelve days were past, and now the seer
Of the great change he saw was drawing near
Informed his King, who read to him the prayers,
And for the end each friendly act prepares,
Then said: "O my Heabani, dearest friend,
I would that I thy body could defend
From thy fierce foe that brings the end to thee.
My friend in battle I may never see
Again, when thou didst nobly stand beside
Me; with my seer and friend I then defied
All foes; and must thou leave thy friend, my seer?
"Alas! my King, I soon shall leave thee here."

COLUMN III

But, oh, my King! to thee I now reveal
A secret that my heart would yet conceal,
To thee, my friend, two visions I reveal:
The first I oft have dreamed beneath some spell
Of night, when I enwrapped from all the world,
With Self alone communed.
                              Unconscious hurled
By wingèd thought beyond this present life,
I seeming woke in a Dark World where rife
Was Nothingness,--a darksome mist it seemed,
All eke was naught;--no light for me there gleamed;
And floating 'lone, which way I turned, saw naught;
Nor felt of substance 'neath my feet, nor fraught
With light was Space around; nor cheerful ray
Of single star. The sun was quenched; or day
Or night, knew not. No hands had I, nor feet,
Nor head, nor body, all was void. No heat
Or cold I felt, no form could feel or see;
And naught I knew but conscious entity.
No boundary my being felt, or had;
And speechless, deaf, and blind, and formless, sad,
I floated through dark space,--a conscious blank!
No breath of air my spirit moved; I sank
I knew not where, till motionless I ceased
At last to move, and yet I could not rest,
Around me spread the Limitless, and Vast.
My cheerless, conscious spirit,--fixed and fast
In some lone spot in space was moveless, stark!
An atom chained by forces stern and dark,
With naught around me. Comfortless I lived
In my dread loneliness! Oh, how I grieved!
And thus, man's fate in Life and Death is solved
With naught but consciousness, and thus involved

All men in hopes that no fruition have?
And this alone was all that death me gave?
That all had vanished, gone from me that life
Could give, and left me but a blank, with strife
Of rising thoughts, and vain regrets, to float;--
Away from life and light, be chained remote!

Oh, how my spirit longed for some lone crag
To part the gloom beneath, and rudely drag

My senses back! or with its shock to end
My dire existence;--to oblivion send
Me quickly! How I strove to curse, and break
That soundless Void, with shrieks or cries, to wake
That awful silence which around me spread!
In vain! in vain! all but my soul was dead.
And then my spirit soundless cried within:
"Oh, take me! take me back to Earth again!"
For tortures of the flesh were bliss and joy
To such existence! Pain can never cloy
The smallest thrill of earthly happiness!
'Twas joy to live on earth in pain! I'll bless
Thee, gods, if I may see its fields I've trod
To kiss its fragrant flowers, and clasp the sod
Of mother Earth, that grand and beauteous world!
From all its happiness, alas! was hurled
My spirit,--then in frenzy--I awoke!
Great Bel! a dream it was! as vanished smoke
It sped! and I sprang from my couch and prayed
To all the gods, and thus my soul allayed.
And then with blessings on my lips, I sought
My couch, and dropped away in blissful thought
In dream the second:
     Then the Silver Sky
Came to me. Near the Stream of Life I lie:
My couch the rarest flowers; and music thrills
My soul! How soft and sweet it sounds from rills
And streams, and feathered songsters in the trees
Of Heaven's fruits!--e'en all that here doth please
The heart of man was there. In a dear spot
I lay, 'mid olives, spices, where was wrought

A beauteous grotto; and beside me near,
Were friends I loved; and one both near and dear
With me reclined, in blissful converse, sweet
With tender thoughts.
    Our joy was lull, complete!
The ministering spirits there had spread
Before us all a banquet on the mead,
With Heaven's food and nectar for our feast;
And oh, so happy! How our joy increased
As moments flew, to years without an end!
To Courts Refulgent there we oft did wend.

Beside a silver lake, a holy fane
There stood within the centre of the plain,
High built on terraces, with walls of gold,
Where palaces and mansions there enfold
A temple of the gods, that stands within
'Mid feathery palms and *gesdin*, bowers green,

The city rises to a dizzy height,
With jewelled turrets flashing in the light,
Grand mansions piled on mansions rising high
Until the glowing summits reach the sky.
A cloud of myriad wings, e'er fills the sky,
As doves around their nests on earth here fly;
The countless millions of the souls on earth,
The gods have brought to light from mortal birth,
Are carried there from the dark world of doom;
For countless numbers more there still is room.
Through trailing vines my Love and I oft wind,
With arms of love around each other twined.
This day, we passed along the Stream of Life,
Through blooming gardens, with sweet odors rife;
Beneath the ever-ripening fruits we walk,
Along dear paths, and sweetly sing, or talk,
While warbling birds around us fly in view,
From bloom to bloom with wings of every hue;
And large-eyed deer, no longer wild, us pass,
With young gazelles, and kiss each other's face.
We now have reached the stately stairs of gold,
The city of the gods, here built of old.

The pearlèd pillars rise inlaid divine,
With lotus delicately traced with vine
In gold and diamonds, pearls, and unknown gems,
That wind to capital with blooming stems
Of lilies, honeysuckles, and the rose.
An avenue of columns in long rows
Of varied splendor, leads to shining courts
Where skilful spirit hands with perfect arts
Have chiselled glorious forms magnificent,
With ornate skill and sweet embellishment.
Their golden sculpture view on every hand,
Or carvèd images in pearl that stand
In clusters on the floor, or in long rows;
And on the walls of purest pearl there glows
The painting of each act of kindest deed
Each soul performs on earth;--is there portrayed.

The scenes of tenderness and holy love,
There stand and never end, but onward move,
And fill the galleries of Heaven with joy,
And ever spirit artist hands employ.
The holiest deeds are carved in purest gold,
Or richest gems, and there are stored of old;
Within the inner court a fountain stood,
Of purest diamond moulded, whence there flowed
Into a golden chalice,--trickling cool,
The nectar of the gods,--a sparkling pool,

That murmuring sank beneath an emerald vase
That rested underneath;--the fountain's base.

We entered then an arcade arching long
Through saph'rine galleries, and heard the song
That swelling came from temples hyaline;
And passed through lazite courts and halls divine,
While dazzling glories brighter round us shone.
How sweet then came the strains! with grander tone!
And, oh, my King! I reached the gates of pearl
That stood ajar, and heard the joyous whirl
That thrilled the sounding domes and lofty halls,
And echoed from the shining jasper walls.

I stood within the gate, and, oh, my friend,
Before that holy sight I prone did bend,
And hid my face upon the jacinth stairs.
A shining god raised me, and bade my fears
Be flown, and I beheld the glorious throne
Of crystaled light; with rays by man unknown.
The awful god there sat with brows sublime,
With robes of woven gold, and diadem
That beamed with blazing splendor o'er his head.
I thus beheld the god with presence dread,
The King of Kings, the Ancient of the Days,
While music rose around with joyous praise.
With awful thunders how they all rejoice!
And sing aloud with one commingled voice!

What happiness it was to me, my King!
From bower to temple I went oft to sing,
Or spread my wings above the mount divine,
And viewed the fields from heights cerulean.
Those songs still linger on dear memory's ear,
And tireless rest upon me, ever cheer.
But from the Happy Fields, alas! I woke,
And from my sight the Heavenly vision broke;
But, oh, my King, it all was but a dream!
I hope the truth is such, as it did seem
If it is true that such a Heavenly Land
Exists with happiness so glorious, grand,
Within that haven I would happy be!
But it, alas! is now denied to me.
For, oh, my King, to Hades I must go,
My wings unfold to fly to Realms of Woe;
In darkness to that other world unknown,
Alas! from joyous earth my life has flown.

Farewell, my King, my love thou knowest well;
I go the road; in Hades soon shall dwell;
To dwelling of the god Irkalla fierce,
To walls where light for me can never pierce,
The road from which no soul may e'er return,
Where dust shall wrap me round, my body urn,

Where sateless ravens float upon the air,
Where light is never seen, or enters there,
Where I in darkness shall be crowned with gloom;
With crownèd heads of earth who there shall come
To reign with Anu's favor or great Bel's,
Then sceptreless are chained in their dark cells
With naught to drink but Hades' waters there,
And dream of all the past with blank despair.
Within that world, I too shall ceaseless moan,
Where dwell the lord and the unconquered one,
And seers and great men dwell within that deep,
With dragons of those realms we all shall sleep;
Where King Etana and god Ner doth reign
With Allat, the dark Under-World's great queen,
Who reigns o'er all within her regions lone,
The Mistress of the Fields, her mother, prone
Before her falls, and none her face withstands
But I will her approach, and take her hands,
And she will comfort me in my dread woe.
Alas! through yonder void I now must go!
My hands I spread! as birds with wings I fly!
Descend! descend! beneath that awful sky!
The seer falls in the arms of Izdubar,
And he is gone;--'tis clay remaineth here,

COLUMN IV

THE GRIEF OF THE KING OVER THE LOSS OF HIS SEER, AND HIS PRAYER TO THE MOON-GOD, WHO ANSWERS HIS PRAYER WITH A VISION

The King weeps bitterly with flowing tears
Above his seer when from him disappears
The last faint breath; and then in deepest woe
He cries: "And through that desert must I go?
Heabani, thou to me wast like the gods;
Oh, how I loved thee! must thou turn to clods?
Through that dread desert must I ride alone;

And leave thee here, Heabani, lying prone?
Alas, I leave thee in this awful place,
To find our Khasisadra, seek his face,
The son of Ubara-tutu, the seer;
Oh, how can I, my friend, thus leave thee here?
This night through those dark mountains I must go,
I can no longer bear this awful woe:
If I shall tarry here, I cannot sleep.
O Sin, bright moon-god, of yon awful deep!
I pray to thee upon my face, oh, hear
My prayer! my supplications bring thou near
To all the gods! grant thou to me,--e'en me,
A heart of strength and will to worship thee.

Oh, is this death like that the seer hath dreamed?
Perhaps the truth then on his spirit gleamed!
If Land of Silver Sky is but a myth,
The other dream is true! e'en all he saith!
Oh, tell me, all ye sparkling stars,
That wing above thy glorious flight,
    And feel not Nature's jars;
But grandly, sweetly fling thy light
To our bright world beneath serene,
    Hath mortals on thee known
Or viewed beyond,--that great Unseen,
Their future fate by gods been shown?

Oh, hear me, all ye gods on high!
To gods who love mankind I pray,
Despairing, oh, I cry!
Oh, drive these doubts and fears away!
And yet--and yet, what truths have we?
O wondrous mortal, must thou die?
Beyond this end thou canst not see,
O Life! O Death! O mystery!

The body still is here, with feeling dead!
And sight is gone!--and hearing from his dead,
Nor taste, nor smell, nor warmth, nor breath of life!
Where is my seer? Perhaps, his spirit rife

E'en now in nothingness doth wander lone!
In agony his thoughts! with spirit prone!
In dread despair!--If conscious then, O gods!
He spake the truth!--His body to the clods
Hath turned! By this we feel, or hear, or see,
And when 'tis gone,--exist?--in agony!
To Hades hath he gone? as he hath thought!
Alas, the thought is torture, where have wrought

The gods their fearful curse! Ah, let me think!
The Silver Sky? Alas, its shining brink
He hath not crossed. The wrathful gods deny
Him entrance! Where, oh, where do spirits fly
Whom gods have cursed? Alas, he is condemned
To wander lone in that dark world, contemned
And from the Light of Happy Fields is barred!
Oh, why do gods thus send a fate so hard,
And cruel? O dear moon-god, moon-god Sin!
My seer hath erred. Receive his soul within
To joys prepared for gods and men! Though seer
He was, he immortality did fear,
As some unknown awakening in space.
Oh, turn upon him thy bright blessèd face!
He was my friend! O moon-god, hear my prayer!
Imploring thee, doth pray thine Izdubar!"

And lo! a vision breaks before his eyes!
The moon-god hides the shadows of the skies,
And sweeps above with his soft, soothing light
That streams around his face; he drives the night
Before his rays, and with his hands sweet peace
He spreads through all the skies; and Strife doth cease!
A girdle spans the Heavens with pure light
That shines around the River of the Night,
Within the circling rays a host appears!
The singers of the skies, as blazing spheres!
Hark! Hear their harps and lyres that sweetly sound!
They sing! Oh, how the glowing skies resound!

      "O King of Light and joy and Peace,
        Supreme thy love shall ever reign;

      Oh, can our songs of bliss here cease?
        Our souls for joy cannot restrain,
        Sweep! Sweep thy lyres again!

      The former things --are passed away,
        Which we on earth once knew below;
      And in this bright eternal day
        We happiness alone can know
        Where bliss doth ever flow."

COLUMN V

THE KING BURIES HIS SEER IN THE CAVE, AND CONTINUING HIS JOURNEY, HE MEETS TWO FIERY GIANTS WHO GUIDE THE SUN IN THE HEAVENS--THEY MAKE MERRY OVER THE KING, AND DIRECT HIM ON HIS WAY

The King within the cave his seer entombs,
And mourning sadly from the cavern comes;
The entrance closes with the rocks around,
Again upon his journey he is bound.
But soon within the mountains he is lost
Within the darkness,--as some vessel tost
Upon the trackless waves of unknown seas,
But further from the awful cavern flees.
The morning breaks o'er crags and lonely glens,
And he dismayed, the awful wild now scans.
He reins his steed and wondering looks around,
And sees of every side a mystic ground.
Before him stands the peak of Mount Masu,
The cliffs and crags forlorn his eyes swift view,
And cedars, pines, among the rocks amassed,
That weirdly rise within the mountain fast.
Hark! hear that dreadful roaring all around!
What nameless horror thrills the shaking ground?

The King in terror stares! and see! his steed
Springs back! wild snorting,--trembling in his dread.
Behold! behold those forms there blazing bright!
Fierce flying by the earth with lurid light;
Two awful spirits, demons, or fierce gods,
With roaring thunders spring from their abodes!
From depths beneath the earth the monsters fly,
And upward lift their awful bodies high,
Yet higher!--higher! till their crests are crowned
By Heaven's gates; thus reaching from the ground
To heights empyrean, while downward falls
Each form, extending far 'neath Hades' walls.
And see! each god as molten metal gleams,
While sulphurous flame from hell each monster climbs!
Two fiery horrors reaching to the skies
While wrathful lightning from each monster flies!

Hell's gate they guard with Death's remorseless face,
And hurl the sun around the realms of space
E'en swifter than the lightning, while it goes
Along its orbit, guided by their blows.
Dire tempests rise above from their dread blows,
And ever round a starry whirlwind glows;

The countless stars thus driven whirl around,
With all the circling planets circling round.

The King astounded lifts his staring eyes,
Into his face gray fear, with terror flies;
As they approach, his thoughts the King collects,
Thus over him one of the gods reflects.
"Who cometh yonder with the form of gods?"
The second says: "He comes from man's abodes,
But with a mortal's feebleness he walks;
Behold upon the ground alone he stalks."

One lifts his mighty arm across the sky,
And strikes the sun as it goes roaring by
The fiery world with whiter heat now glows,
While a vast flood of flame behind it flows,
That curling, forms bright comets, meteors,

And planets multiplies, and blazing stars;
The robe of flames spreads vast across the sky.
Adorned with starry gems that sparkling fly
Upon the ambient ether forming suns
That through new orbits sing their orisons;
Their pealing thunders rend the trembling sky,
The endless anthem of eternity.

The monster turning to the King then says,
When nearer now his awful form doth blaze:
"So thus you see, my son, the gods are strong,
And to provoke great power, is foolish, wrong;
But whither goest thou, thou sad-eyed King,
What message hast thou;--to us here would bring?"

The King now prostrate to the monsters prayed:
"Ye gods or demons, I within your glade
Of horrors, have unwilling come to seek
Our Khasisadra, who a spell can make
To turn the anger of the gods away.
Immortal lives the seer beside the sea,
He knoweth death and life, all secret things;
And this alone your servant to you brings.
The goddess sought my hand, which I denied,
And Anu's fury thus I have defied;
This all my troubles caused, show me the way
To Khasisadra, this I ask and pray."

The god's vast face broke out with wondrous smiles,
And laughing, ripples rolled along for miles;
His mouth wide opened its abyss and yawned,

As earthquake gulf, far spreading through the ground.
His roaring laughter shakes the earth around,
"Ho! ho! my son! so you at last have found
The Queen can hate, as well as love her friends,
And on thy journey Ishtar's love thee sends?
A mortal wise thou wast, to her refuse,
For she can do with man what she may choose.
A mortal's love, in truth, is wondrous strong,
A glorious thing it is, Life's ceaseless song!

Within a cave upon the mountain side,
Thou there thy footsteps must to Hades guide,
Twelve *kaspu* go to yonder mountain gates,
A heart like thine may well defy the fates.
A darkness deep profound doth ever spread
Within those regions black,--Home of the Dead.
Go, Izdubar! within this land of Mas,
Thy road doth lead, and to the west doth pass,
And may the maidens sitting by the walls
Refresh thee, lead thee to the Happy Halls."

The path they take behind the rising sun
The setting sun they pass,--with wings have flown
The scorpion men, within wide space have gone,
Thus from his sight the monsters far have flown.

COLUMN VI

IZDUBAR ENTERS HADES--THE SONG OF THE DALKHI IN THE CAVERN OF HORRORS--THE KING PASSES THROUGH HADES TO THE GARDEN OF THE GODS, AND SEES THE WONDERFUL FOUNTAIN OF LIFE'S WATERS

In a weird passage to the Under-World,
Where demon shades sit with their pinions furled
Along the cavern's walls with poisonous breath,
In rows here mark the labyrinths of Death.
The King with torch upraised, the pathway finds,
Along the way of mortal souls he winds,
Where shades sepulchral, soundless rise amid
Dark gulfs that yawn, and in the blackness hide
Their depths beneath the waves of gloomy lakes
And streams that sleep beneath the sulphurous flakes
That drift o'er waters bottomless, and chasms;
Where moveless depths receive Life's dying spasms.

Here Silence sits supreme on a drear throne
Of ebon hue, and joyless reigns alone
O'er a wide waste of blackness,--solitude
Black, at her feet, there sleeps the awful flood
Of mystery which grasps all mortal souls,
Where grisly horrors sit with crests of ghouls,
And hateless welcome with their eyes of fire
Each soul;--remorseless lead to terrors dire;
And ever, ever crown the god of Fate;
And there, upon her ebon throne she sate
The awful fiend, dark goddess Mam-mitu,
Who reigns through all these realms of La-Atzu.

But hark! what are these sounds within the gloom?
And see! long lines of torches nearer come!
And now within a recess they have gone;
The King must pass their door! perhaps some one
Of them may see him! turn the hags of gloom
Upon him, as he goes by yonder room!
He nearer comes, and peers within; and see!
A greenish glare fills all the cave! and he
Beholds a blaze beneath a cauldron there;
Coiled, yonder lie the Dragons of Despair;
And lo! from every recess springs a form
Of shapeless horror! now with dread alarm
He sees the flitting forms wild whirling there,
And awful wailings come of wild despair:
But hark! the *dal-khis'* song rings on the air!
With groans and cries they shriek their mad despair.

Oh, fling on earth, ye demons dark,
  Your madness, hate, and fell despair,
And fling your darts at each we mark,
  That we may welcome victims here.

Then sing your song of hate, ye fiends,
  And hurl your pestilential breath,
Till every soul before us bends,
  And worship here the god of Death.

In error still for e'er and aye,
  They see not, hear not many things;
The unseen forces do not weigh,
  And each an unknown mystery brings.

In error still for e'er and aye,
  They delve for phantom shapes that ride
Across their minds alone,--and they
  But mock the folly of man's pride.

In error still for e'er and aye!
  They learn but little all their lives,
And Wisdom ever wings her way,
  Evading ever,--while man strives!

But hark! another song rings through the gloom,
  And, oh, how sweet the music far doth come!
Oh, hear it, all ye souls in your despair,
  For joy it brings to sorrowing ones e'en here!

"There is a Deep Unknown beyond,
  That all things hidden well doth weigh!
On man's blind vision rests the bond
  Of error still for e'er and aye!

But to the mighty gods, oh, turn
  For truth to lead you on your way,
And wisdom from their tablets learn,
  And ever hope for e'er and aye!"

And see! the hags disperse within the gloom,
As those sweet sounds resound within the room;
And now a glorious light doth shine around,
Their rays of peace glide o'er the gloomy ground.
And lo! 'tis Papsukul, our god of Hope,--
With cheerful face comes down the fearful slope
Of rugged crags, and blithely strides to where
Our hero stands, amid the poisonous air,
And says:
        "Behold, my King, that glorious Light
That shines beyond! and eye no more this sight

Of dreariness, that only brings despair,
For phantasy of madness reigneth here!"
The King in wonder carefully now eyes
The messenger divine with great surprise,
And says:
        "But why, thou god of Hope, do I
Thus find thee in these realms of agony?
This World around me banishes thy feet
From paths that welcome here the god of Fate
And blank despair, and loss irreparable.
Why comest thou to woe immeasurable?"

"You err, my King, for hope oft rules despair;
I ofttimes come to reign with darkness here;
When I am gone, the god of Fate doth reign;
When I return, I soothe these souls again."
"So thus you visit all these realms of woe,

To torture them with hopes they ne'er can know?
Avaunt! If this thy mission is on Earth
Or Hell, thou leavest after thee but dearth!"
"Not so, my King! behold yon glorious sphere,
Where gods at last take all these souls from here!
Adieu! thou soon shalt see the World of Light,
Where joy alone these souls will e'er delight."

The god now vanishes away from sight,
The hero turns his face toward the light;
Nine *kaspu* walks, till weird the rays now gleam,
As *zi-mu-ri* behind the shadows stream.
He sees beyond, umbrageous grots and caves,
Where odorous plants entwine their glistening leaves.
And lo! the trees bright flashing gems here bear!
And trailing vines and flowers do now appear,
That spread before his eyes a welcome sight,
Like a sweet dream of some mild summer night.
But, oh! his path leads o'er that awful stream,
Across a dizzy arch 'mid sulphurous steam
That covers all the grimy bridge with slime.
He stands perplexed beside the waters grime,
Which sluggish move adown the limbo black,
With murky waves that writhe demoniac,--

As ebon serpents curling through the gloom
And burl their inky crests, that silent come
Toward the yawning gulf, a tide of hate;
And sweep their dingy waters to Realms of Fate.

He cautious climbs the slippery walls of gloom,
And dares not look beneath, lest Fate should come;
He enters now the stifling clouds that creep
Around the causeway, while its shadows sleep
Upon the stream that sullen moves below,--

He slips!--and drops his torch! it far doth glow
Beneath him on the rocks! Alas, in vain
He seeks a path to bring it back again.
It moves! snatched by a *dal-khu's* hand it flies
Away within the gloom, then falling dies
Within those waters black with a loud hiss
That breaks the silence of that dread abyss.

He turns again, amid the darkness gropes,
And careful climbs the cragged, slimy slopes,
And now he sees, oh, joy! the light beyond!
He springs! he flies along the glowing ground,
And joyous dashes through the waving green

That lustrous meets his sight with rays serene,
Where trees pure amber from their trunks distil,
Where sweet perfumes the groves and arbors fill,
Where zephyrs murmur odors from the trees,
And sweep across the flowers, carrying bees
With honey laden for their nectar store;
Where humming sun-birds upward flitting soar
O'er groves that bear rich jewels as their fruit,
That sparkling tingle from each youngling shoot,
And fill the garden with a glorious blaze
Of chastened light and tender thrilling rays.
He glides through that enchanted mystic world,
O'er streams with beds of gold that sweetly twirled
With woven splendor 'neath the blaze of gems
That crown each tree with glistening diadems.
The sounds of streams are weft with breezes, chant
Their arias with trembling leaves,--the haunt

Of gods! O how the tinkling chorus rings!
With rhythms of the unseen rustling wings
Of souls that hover here where joy redeems
Them with a happiness that ever gleams.

The hero stands upon a damasked bed
Of flowers that glow beneath his welcome tread,
And softly sink with 'luring odors round,
And beckon him to them upon the ground.
Amid rare pinks and violets he lies,
And one sweet pink low bending near, he eyes.
With tender petals thrilling on its stem,
It lifts its fragrant face and says to him,
"Dear King, wilt thou love me as I do thee?
We love mankind, and when a mortal see
We give our fragrance to them with our love,
Their love for us our inmost heart doth move."
The King leans down his head, it kissing, says,
"Sweet beauty, I love thee? with thy sweet face?
My heart is filled with love for all thy kind.
I would that every heart thy love should find."
The fragrant floweret thrills with tenderness,
With richer fragrance answers his caress.
He kisses it again and lifts his eyes,
And rises from the ground with glad surprise.

And see! the glorious spirits clustering round!
They welcome him with sweet melodious sound.
We hear their golden instruments of praise,
As they around him whirl a threading maze;
In great delight he views their beckoning arms,

And lustrous eyes, and perfect, moving forms.
And see! he seizes one bright, charming girl,
As the enchanting ring doth nearer whirl;
He grasps her in his arms, and she doth yield
The treasure of her lips, where sweets distilled
Give him a joy without a taint of guilt.
It thrills his heart-strings till his soul doth melt,
A kiss of chastity, and love, and fire,
A joy that few can dare to here aspire.

The beauteous spirit has her joy, and flees
With all her sister spirits 'neath the trees.
And lo! the *gesdin* shining stands,
With crystal branches in the golden sands,
In this immortal garden stands the tree,
With trunk of gold, and beautiful to see.
Beside a sacred fount the tree is placed,
With emeralds and unknown gems is graced,
Thus stands, the prince of emeralds, Elam's tree,
As once it stood, gave Immortality
To man, and bearing fruit, there sacred grew,
Till Heaven claimed again Fair Eridu.

The hero now the wondrous fountain eyes;
Its beryl base to ruby stem doth rise,
To emerald and sapphire bands that glow,
Where the bright curvings graceful outward flow;
Around the fountain to its widest part,
The wondrous lazite bands now curling start
And mingle with bright amethyst that glows,
To a broad diamond band,--contracting grows
To *uk-ni* stone, turquoise, and clustering pearls,
Inlaid with gold in many curious curls
Of twining vines and tendrils bearing birds,
Among the leaves and blooming flowers, that words
May not reveal, such loveliness in art,
With fancies spirit hands can only start
From plastic elements before the eye,
And mingle there the charms of empery.
Beneath two diamond doves that shining glow
Upon the summit, the bright waters flow,
With aromatic splendors to the skies,
While glistening colors of the rainbow rise.

Here ends the tablet, "When the hero viewed
The fountain which within the garden stood."

TABLET VIII

COLUMN I

THE KING'S ADVENTURE AT THE GATE OF THE GARDEN OF THE GODS WITH THE TWO MAIDENS--ONE OF THEM LEADS HIM INTO THE HAPPY HALLS-- SONGS OF THE SABITU AND ZI-SI.

A gate half opened shows the silvery sea
Yet distant shining lambent on his way.
And now he sees young Siduri, whose breast
Infuses life; all nature she hath blest,
Whose lips are flames, her arms are walls of fire,
Whose love yields pleasures that can never tire,
She to the souls who joy on earth here miss,
Grants them above a holier, purer bliss.
The maiden sits within a holy shrine
Beside the gate with lustrous eyes divine,
And beckons to the King, who nearer comes,
And near her glows the Happy Palace domes.

And lo! 'tis she his lips have fondly kissed
Within the garden, when like fleeing mist
She disappeared with the bright spirit Seven,
The Sabit, who oft glide from earth to Heaven.
And lo I one of the Seven, Sabitu,
Emerging from the gate doth jealous view
The coming hero who hath kissed her mate,
She angry springs within to close the gate,
And bars it, enters then the inner halls,
And Izdubar to her now loudly calls,
"O Sabitu! what see-est thou, my maid?
Of Izdubar is Sabitu afraid?
Thy gate thou barrest thus before my face.
Quick, open for me! or I'll force the brass!"
The maid now frightened opens wide the door.

The Sar and Siduri now tread the floor
Of the bright palace where sweet joy doth reign.
Through crystal halls 'neath golden roofs the twain
Next go within a lofty ceilinged hall,
With shining pearlèd columns, golden wall,
And purple silken hangings at each door,
With precious gems inlaid upon the floor;
Where couches grand are spread for one to rest
Beneath the softened rays that sweet invest
The senses with a thrill of happiness;
Where Siduri with joy all souls doth bless.
The maid sits on a couch and turns her face
Toward the King with that immortal grace
That love to gods and men will e'er bestow.
Their eyes now mingling with a happy glow,
The maiden sweetly says: "Where wouldst thou go?
Within these Happy Halls we joy but know,
And if thou wilt, my King, my heart is thine!
Our love will ever bring us bliss divine."

"Alas, my maid, thy love to me is dear,
And sad am I that I must go from here.
I came from Erech by advice from one
I loved more than thou canst e'er know, but gone
From me is my Heabani, faithful seer.
Across a desert waste have I come here,
And he has there to dust returned,--to dust--
O how the love of my friend I did trust!
I would that we had never started here,
I now must find the great immortal seer."

The maiden turns her glowing eyes on him,
Replies: "My King, thou knowest joy may gleam,
Take courage, weary heart, and sing a song!
The hour of sorrow can never be long;
The day will break, and flood thy soul with joy,
And happiness thy heart will then employ!
Each day must end with all its sorrow, woe,
Oh, sing with me, dear heart! I love thee so!"
And lo! the curtains flung aside, now comes

The joyous Sabitu from yonder rooms,
And gathering round, a song they gayly sing,
Oh, how with music the bright walls now ring!
If evil thou hast done, my King,

Oh, pray! oh, pray!
And to the gods thy offerings bring,
And pray! and pray!

The sea is roaring at thy feet,
The storms are coming, rain and sleet;
        To all the gods,
Oh, pray to them I oh, pray!

Chorus

        To all the gods,
Oh, pray to them! oh, pray!

Thy city we will bless, O Sar!
        With joy, with joy!
And prosper thee in peace and war
        With joy, with joy!
And bless thee every day and night,
Thy kingly robes keep pure and bright;
        Give thee bright dreams,
O glorious king of war!

Chorus

        Give thee bright dreams,
O glorious king of war!

And if thy hand would slay thy foes
        In war, in war!
With thee returning victory goes
        In war, in war!
We grant thee victory, my King;
Like marshes swept by storms, we bring
        Our power to thee
With victory in war!

Chorus

        Our power to thee
With victory in war!

And if thou wouldst the waters pass,
        The sea, the sea!
We'll go with thee in every place,
        With thee, with thee!
To Hea's halls and glorious throne,
Where he unrivalled reigns alone,
        To Hea go
Upon his throne of snow.

To Hea go
Upon his throne of snow.

And if thine anger rules thy heart
  As fire, as fire!
And thou against thy foes would start
  With ire, with ire!
Against thy foes thy heart be hard,
And all their land with fire be scarred,
  Destroy thy foes!
Destroy them in thine ire!

Chorus

Destroy thy foes!
Destroy them in thine ire!

And lo! young Siduri hath disappeared,
And with the Zisi crowned she now appeared;
The corn-gods in a crescent round their queen,
She waves before the king her Nusku green,
And sings with her sweet voice a joyful lay,
And all the Zisi join the chorus gay:

A heifer of the corn am I,
  Kara! Kara!
Yoked with the kine we gayly fly,
  Kara! Kara!
The ploughman's hand is strong and drives
The glowing soil, the meadow thrives!
  Before the oxen
Sa-lum-mat-u na-si.

Chorus

Before the oxen
Sa-lum-mat-u na-si.

The harvesters are in the corn!
  Kara! Kara!
Our feet are flying with the morn,
  Kara! Kara!
We bring thee wealth! it is thine own!
The grain is ripe! oh, cut it down!
  The yellow grain
Sa-lum-mat-u na-si.

Chorus

The yellow grain
Sa-lum-mat-u na-si.

The fruit of death, oh, King, taste it not!
        Taste not! taste not!
With fruit of Life the land is fraught
        Around! around!
The fruit of Life we give to thee
And happiness, oh, ever see.
        All joy is thine
Through Earth and Heaven's bound.

Chorus

All joy is thine
Through Earth and Heaven's bound.

Our corn immortal there is high
        And ripe! and ripe!
And ever ripens 'neath that sky
        As gold! as gold!
Our corn is bearded, thus 'tis known,
And ripens quickly when 'tis grown.
        Be joy with thee,
Our love around thee fold!

Chorus

Be joy with thee,
Our love around thee fold!

Our King from us now goes, now goes!
        Away! away!
His royal robe behind him glows
        Afar! afar!
Across the waves where Hea reigns
The waters swollen he soon gains!
        To our great seer,
He sails to him afar!

Chorus

To our great seer,
He sails to him afar!

And he will reach that glorious land
    Away! away!
Amid our fruit-trees he will stand
    That day! that day!
Our fruit so sweet the King will eat,
Nor bitter mingle with the sweet.
    In our seer's land
That glows afar away!

Chorus

    In our seer's land
That glows afar away!

The singing spirits from them fled, and he
Alone stood thinking by young Siduri.

The King leaned on his bow, and eyed the maid,
A happy look came in his eyes,--and fled,
For lo! the curtain quick aside is pushed,
And Sabitu within upon them rushed.
She stately glides across the shining floor,
And eyes them both, then turns toward the door.
But Izdubar is equal to the task,
With grace now smiling, of the maid doth ask:
"O Sabitu! wouldst thou tell me the way
To Khasisadra? for I go this day.
If I the sea may cross, how shall I go?
Or through the desert? thou the path mayst know."
The maiden startled looks upon his face,
And thus she answers him with queenly grace:
"So soon must go? Thou canst not cross the sea,
For thou wilt perish in the waves that way.
Great Samas once the way of me did ask,
And I forbade him, but the mighty task
He undertook, and crossed the mighty deep,
Where Death's dark waters lie in wait asleep:
His mighty car of gold swept through the skies,
With fiery chargers now he daily flies.
When I approach thee, thou from me wouldst flee?
But if thou must so soon thus go, the sea
Perhaps thou too canst cross, if thou wilt 'void
Death's waters, which relentless ever glide.
But Izdubar, Ur-Hea, here hath come!
The boatman of the seer, who to his home
Returns. He with an axe in yonder woods
A vessel builds to cross the raging floods.

If thou desirest not to cross with him,
We here will welcome thee through endless time;
But if thou goest, may they see thy face
Thou seekest,--welcome thee, and thy heart bless."

COLUMN II

THE KING ON LEAVING THE HAPPY HALLS MEETS UR-HEA, THE BOATMAN OF THE SEER KHASISADRA--THEY BUILD A SHIP AND EMBARK ON AN UNKNOWN SEA, AND ON THEIR VOYAGE PASS THROUGH THE WATERS OF DEATH

And Izdubar turned from the Halls and goes
Toward a fountain in the park, whence flows
A merry stream toward the wood. He finds
An axe beside the fount, and thoughtful winds,
Through groves of sandal-wood and mastic-trees
And algum, umritgana. Now he sees
The sig-a-ri and ummakana, pines,
With babuaku; and ri-wood brightly shines
Among the azuhu; all precious woods
That man esteems are grown around, each buds
Continuous in the softened, balmy air.
He stops beneath a musrilkanna where
The pine-trees spread toward the glowing sea,
Wild mingled with the surman, sa-u-ri.

The King, now seated, with himself communes,
Heeds not the warbling of the birds, and tunes
Of gorgeous songsters in the trees around,
But sadly sighing gazes on the ground:
"And I a ship must build; alas! I know
Not how I shall return, if I thus go.
The awful Flood of Death awaits me there,
Wide-stretching from this shore--I know not where."
He rests his chin upon his hand in thought,
Full weary of a life that woe had brought;
He says: "When I remember Siduri,
Whose heart with fondest love would comfort me
Within these Happy Halls, why should I go
To pain and anguish, death, mayhap, and woe?
But will I thus desert my kingdom, throne?
For one I know not! What! my fame alone!
Mine honor should preserve! and royal state!
Alas! this Fame is but a dream of--Fate!

A longing after that which does not cheer
The heart. Applause of men, or thoughtless sneer,
Is naught to me, I am alone! alone!
This Immortality cannot atone
For my hard fate that wrings mine aching heart.
I long for peace and rest, and I must start
And find it, leave these luring bright abodes,--
I seek the immortality of gods.
This Fame of man is not what it doth seem,
It sleeps with all the past, a vanished dream.
My duty calls me to my kingdom, throne!
To Khasisadra go, whose aid alone
Can save my people from an awful fate
That hangs above them, born of Fiends of hate.
And I shall there return without my seer!
I live; and he is dead. Why did I hear
His words advising me to come? Alas!
I sadly all my weary days shall pass;
No one shall love me as my seer, my friend.

But what said Siduri?--There comes an end
At last to sorrow, joy will hopeful spring
On wings of Light! Oh, how my heart will sing!
I bless ye all, ye holy spirits here!
Your songs will linger with me, my heart cheer;
Upon my way I turn with joy again!
How true your joyful song! your memory then
Will keep me hopeful through yon darkened way;
How bright this land doth look beside the sea!"

He looks across the fields; the river glows
And winds beside taprani-trees, and flows
By teberinth and groves of tarpikhi
And ku-trees; curving round green mez-kha-i,
Through beds of flowers, that kiss its waves and spring
Luxuriant,--with songs the groves far ring.
Now thinking of the ship, he turns his eyes,
Toward the fountain,--springs up with surprise!
"'Tis he! the boatman comes! Ur-Hea comes!
And, oh! at last, I'll reach the glistening domes

Of Khasisadra's palaces,--at last
My feet shall rest,--upon that land be placed."

And now Ur-Hea nearer makes his way,
And Izdubar addressing him, doth say:
"Ur-Hea is thy name? from yonder sea
Thou comest, from the seer across the way?"

"Thou speakest truth, great Sar, what wouldst thou have?"
"How shall I Khasisadra reach? The grave
He hath escaped, Immortal lives beyond,
For I to him upon my way am bound;
Shall I the waters cross or take my way
Through yon wide desert, for I start this day?"

"Across the sea we go, for I with thee
Return to him,--I know the winding way.
Thine axe of bronze with precious stones inlaid
With mine, we'll use beneath the pine-trees' shade."

And now, within the grove a ship they made,
Complete and strong as wise Ur-Hea bade.
They fell the pines five *gar* in length, and hew
The timbers square, and soon construct a new
And buoyant vessel, firmly fixed the mast,
And tackling, sails, and oars make taut and fast.
Thus built, toward the sea they push its prow,
Equipped complete, provisioned, launch it now.
An altar next they raise and thus invoke
The gods, their evil-workings to revoke:

  O Lord of Charms, Illustrious! who gives
Life to the Dead, the Merciful who lives,
And grants to hostile gods of Heaven return,
To homage render, worship thee, and learn

Obedience! Thou who didst create mankind
In tenderness, thy love round us, oh, wind!
The Merciful, the God with whom is Life,
Establish us, O Lord, in darkest strife.
O never may thy truth forgotten be,
May Accad's race forever worship thee."

One month and fifteen days upon the sea,
Thus far the voyagers are on their way;
Now black before them lies a barren shore,
O'ertopped with frowning cliffs, whence comes a roar
Of some dread fury of the elements
That shakes the air and sweeping wrath foments
O'er winds and seas.
                    And see! a yawning cave,
There opens vast into a void dislave,
Where fremèd shadows ride the hueless waves.
Dread Ninazu whose deathless fury craves
For hapless victims lashes with a roar
The mighty seas upon that awful shore.
The Fiends of Darkness gathered lie in wait,

With Mammitu, the goddess of fierce hate,
And Gibil with his spells, and Nibiru
The twin-god of black Fate, and grim Nusku
The keeper of red thunders, and Urbat
The dog of Death, and fiend of Queen Belat;
And Nuk-khu, and the black-browed Ed-hutu
The gods of darkness here with Tsi-lat-tu.

And see! Dark Rimmon o'er a crag alone!
And Gibil with his blasting malisoun,
Above with his dark face maleficent,
Who wields a power o'er men omnipotent
Forlore! forlore! the souls who feel that blast
Which sweeps around that black forbidding coast!
Fierce whirling storms and hurricanes here leap,
With blasting lightnings maltalent and sweep

The furious waves that lash around that shore,
As the fierce whirl of some dread maëlstrom's power!
Above the cavern's arch! see! Ninip stands!
He points within the cave with beckoning hands!
Ur-Hea cries: "My lord! the tablets say,
That we should not attempt that furious way!
Those waters of black death will smite us down!
Within that cavern's depths we will but drown."
"We cannot go but once, my friend, that road,"
The hero said, "'Tis only ghosts' abode!"
"We go, then, Izdubar, its depths will sound,
But we within that gloom will whirl around,
Around, within that awful whirlpool black,--
And once within, we dare not then turn back,--
How many times, my friend, I dare not say,
'Tis written, we within shall make our way."

The foaming tide now grasped them with its power,
And billowed round them with continuous roar;
Away! they whirl! with growing speed, till now
They fly on lightnings' wings and ride the brow
Of maddened tempests o'er the dizzy deep.
So swift they move,--the waves in seeming sleep
Beneath them, whirling there with force unseen.

But see! Updarting with a sulphurous gleen,
The hag of Death leaps on the trembling prow!
Her eyes, of fire and hate, turns on them now!
With famine gaunt, and haggard face of doom,
She sits there soundless in the awful gloom.

"O gods!" shrieked Izdubar in his despair,
Have I the god of Fate at last met here?
Avaunt, thou Fiend! hence to thy pit of Hell!
Hence! hence! and rid me of thy presence fell!"

And see! she nearer comes with deathless ire,
With those fierce, moveless, glaring eyes of fire!
Her wand is raised! she strikes!

             "O gods!" he screams;
He falls beneath that bolt that on them gleams,
And she is gone within the awful gloom.
Hark! hear those screams!
            "Accurst! Accurst thy doom!"
And lo! he springs upon his feet in pain,
And cries:
         "Thy curses, fiend! I hurl again!"
And now a blinding flash disparts the black
And heavy air, a moment light doth break;
And see! the King leans fainting 'gainst the mast,
With glaring eyeballs, clenched hands,--aghast!
Behold! that pallid face and scaly hands!
A leper white, accurst of gods, he stands!
A living death, a life of awful woe,
Incurable by man, his way shall go.
But oh! the seer in all enchantments wise
Will cure him on that shore, or else he dies.

And see! the vessel's prow with shivering turns,
Adown the roaring flood that gapes and churns
Beneath like some huge boiling cauldron black,
Thus whirl they in the slimy cavern's track.
And spirit ravens round them fill the air,
And see! they fly! the cavern sweeps behind!
Away the ship doth ride before the wind!
The darkness deep from them has fled away,
The fiends are gone!--the vessel in the spray
With spreading sails has caught the glorious breeze,
And dances in the light o'er shining seas;
The blissful haven shines upon their way,
The waters of the Dawn sweep o'er the sea!
They proudly ride tip to the glowing sand,
And joyfully the King springs to the land.

COLUMN III

KHASISADRA ON THE SHORE SEES THE VESSEL COMING, AND RETURNING TO
HIS PALACE, SENDS HIS DAUGHTER MUA TO WELCOME IZDUBAR--MEETING OF
THE KING AND SAGE

Beneath a ku-tree Khasisadra eyes
The spreading sea beneath the azure skies,
An agèd youth with features grave, serene,
Matured with godly wisdom; ne'er was seen
Such majesty, nor young, nor old,--a seer
In purpose high. The countenance no fear
Of death has marred, but on his face sublime
The perfect soul has left its seal through time.

"Ah, yes! the dream was clear, the vision true,
I saw him on the ship! Is it in view?
A speck! Ah, yes! He comes! he comes to me
My son from Erech comes across the sea!"
Back to his palace goes the holy seer,
And Mua sends, who now the shore doth near;
As beautiful as Waters of the Dawn,
Comes Mua here, as graceful as a fawn.

The King now standing on the glistening sand,
Beholds the beauteous Mua where she stands,
With hands outstretched in welcome to the King,
"O thou sweet spirit, with thy snowy wing,
Oh, where is Khasisadra in this land?
I seek the aid of his immortal hand."
"Great Sar," said Mua, "hadst thou not a seer,
That thou shouldst come to seek my father here?"

"'Tis true, my daughter dear, a seer had I,
Whom I have lost,--a dire calamity;
By his advice and love I undertake
This journey. But alas! for mine own sake
He fell by perils on this lengthened way;
He was not strong, and feared that he should lay

Himself to rest amid the mountains wild.
He was a warrior, with him I killed
Khumbaba, Elam's king who safely dwelt
Within a forest vast of pines, and dealt
Destruction o'er the plains. We razed his walls--
My friend at last before me dying falls.

Alas! why did my seer attempt to slay
The dragons that we met upon the way,
He slew his foe, and like a lion died.
Ah, me! the cause, when I the gods defied,
And brought upon us all this awful woe;
In sorrow o'er his death, my life must flow!
For this I came to find the ancient seer,
Lead me to him, I pray, if he lives here."

Then Mua leads him through the glorious land
Of matchless splendor, on the border grand
Of those wide Happy Fields that spread afar
O'er beaming hills and vales, where ambient air
With sweetest zephyrs sweeps a grand estrade,
Where softest odors from each flowering glade
Lull every sense aswoon that breathes not bliss
And harmony with World of Blessedness.
'Neath trees of luring fruits she leads the way,
Through paths of flowers where night hath fled away,
A wilderness of varied crystal flowers,
Where fragrance rests o'er clustering, shining bowers.
Each gleaming cup its nectared wine distils,
For spirit lips each chalice ever fills.

Beyond the groves a lucent palace shone
In grandest splendor near an inner zone;
In amethyst and gold divinely rose,
With glories scintillant the palace glows.
A dazzling halo crowns its lofty domes,
And spreading from its summit softly comes
With grateful rays, and floods the balustrades
And golden statues 'neath the high arcades;
A holy palace built by magic hand
With wondrous architecture, portals grand,

And aurine turrets piled to dizzy heights,
Oh, how its glory Izdubar delights!

Beneath majestic arcades carved, they pass,
Up golden steps that shine like polished glass,
Through noble corridors with sculptured walls,
By lofty columns, archways to the halls
Of glories, the bright harbinger of fanes
Of greater splendor of the Heavenly plains.
Beneath an arch of gems the King espies
A form immortal, he who death defies.
Advancing forth the sage his welcome gives,
"'Tis Izdubar who comes to me and lives!"
Embracing him he leads him in a room,

Where many a curious graven tablet, tome,
And scrolls of quaint and old forgotten lore
Have slept within for centuries of yore.
The tablets high are heaped, the alcoves full,
Where truth at last has found a welcome goal.
In wisdom's room, the sage his guest has led,
And seats him till the banquet high is spread;
Of Izdubar he learns his journeys great,
How he for aid has left his throne of state.

The maid now comes, him welcomes to the hall
Of banquets, where are viands liberal,
And fruits, immortal bread, celestial wines
Of vintage old; and when the hero dines,
They lead him to his private chamber room
That overlooks the wondrous garden's bloom
Across the plain and jasper sea divine,
To Heaven's mountains rising sapphirine.
Four beauteous streams of liquid silver lead
Across the plain; the shining sea they feed;
The King reclines upon his couch at rest,
With dreams of happiness alone is blest.

COLUMN IV

THE KING IS CURED BY THE INCANTATIONS OF KHASISADRA AND HE BECOMES IMMORTAL

When Izdubar awakes, they lead the way
To the bright fount beside the jasper sea.
The seer, with Mua and Ur-Hea, stands
Beside the King, who holily lifts his hands
Above an altar where the glowing rays
Of sacred flames are curling; thus he prays:

"Ye glorious stars that shine on high,
Remember me! Oh, hear my cry,
Su-ku-nu, bright Star of the West!
Dil-gan, my patron star, oh, shine!
O Mar-bu-du, whose rays invest
Dear Nipur with thy light divine,
The flames that shines, upon the Waste!
O Papsukul, thou Star of Hope,
Sweet god of bliss, to me, oh, haste,
Before I faint and lifeless drop!
O Adar Star of Ninazu,

Be kind! O Ra-di-tar-tu-khu.
Sweet U-tu-ca-ga-bu, dear Star
With thy pure face that shines afar!

Oh, pardon me! each glorious Star!
Za-ma-ma, hear me! O Za-ma-ma!
Ca-ca-ma u Ca-ca-ma."

   Remember him! O dear Za-ma-ma!
Ca-ca-ma u Ca-ca-ma."

As Izdubar doth end his holy prayer
He kneels, and they now bear his body where
A snowy couch doth rest beneath a shrine
That stands near by the glowing fount divine,
And Khasisadra lifts his holy hands,
His incantation chants, and o'er him stands.

"O Bel, Lord of An-nu-na-ci,
O Nina, Hea's daughter! Zi!
This Incantation aid,
Remember us, Remember!

   Ye tempests of High Heaven, be still!
Ye raging lightnings, oh, he calm!
From this brave man his strength is gone,
Before thee see him lying ill!
Oh, fill with strength his feeble frame,
O Ishtar, shine from thy bright throne!
From him thine anger turn away,
Come from thy glowing mountains, come!
From paths untrod by man, oh, haste!
And bid this man arise this day.
With strength divine as Heaven's dome,
His form make pure and bright and chaste!
The evil curse, oh, drive away!

Go! A-sac-cu-kab-bi-lu, go!
O Nam-ta-ru-lim-nu, oh, fly!
U-tuc-cu-lim-nu from him flow!
A-lu-u-lim-nu, hence! away!
E-ci-mu-lim-nu, go! thou fiend!
Fly, Gal-lu-u-lim-nu, afar!
Fly from his head! his life! I send
Thee, fiend! depart from Izdubar!
Go from his forehead, breast, and heart,
And feet! Avaunt! thou fiend! depart!

Oh, from the Curse, Thou Spirit High!
And Spirit of the Earth, come nigh!
Protect him, may his spirit fly!
O Spirit of the Lord of Lands,
And Goddess of the Earthly Lands,
Protect him! raise with strength his hands!

Oh, make him as the Holy Gods,
His body, limbs, like thine Abodes,
And like the Heavens may he shine!
And like the Earth with rays divine!
Quick! with the khis-ib-ta to bring
High Heaven's Charm--bind round his brow!
The sis-bu place around his hands!
And let the sab-u-sat bright cling!
The mus-u-kat lay round him now,
And wrap his feet with rad-bat-bands,
And open now his zik-a-man
The sis-bu cover, and his hands
The bas-sat place around his form!
From baldness and disease, this man
Cleanse, make him whole, head, feet, and hands!

O Purity, breathe thy sweet charm!

Restore his health and make his skin
Shine beautifully, beard and hair
Restore! make strong with might his loins!
And may his body glorious shine
As the bright gods!--

       Ye winds him bear!
Immortal flesh to his soul joins!

Thou Spirit of this man! arise!
Come forth with joy! Come to the skies!"

And lo! his leprosy has fled away!
He stands immortal,--purged! released from clay!

COLUMN V

IZDUBAR FALLS IN LOVE WITH MUA, AND OFFERS HER HIS HAND

"O Mua! thou bright Waters of the Dawn!
Oh, where art thou?" one cries as he doth run
Through the bright garden. See! 'tis Izdubar!
Immortal! glorious! our King of War!
And now in love is seeking Mua here.
He scarcely treads the ground as he comes near;
A glow of youth immortal on his cheek,
A form that sorrow, death, will never seek
Within these Happy Fields, his eyes with light
That Love alone may give, show his delight.

A dazzling pillared vista round him shines,
Where golden columns bear the bowering shrines,
With gemmèd domes that clustering round him rise,
'Mid fruit-trees, flashing splendors to the skies.
He goes through silver grots along a zone,
And now he passes yonder blazing throne,
O'er diamond pavements, passes shining seats
Whereon the high and holy conclave meets
To rule the empires vast that spread away
To utmost bounds in all their vast array.
Around the whole expanse grand cestes spread
O'er paths sidereal unending lead.
As circling wheels within a wheel they shine,
Enveloping the Fields with light divine.
A noontide glorious of shining stars,
Where humming music rings from myriad cars,
Where pinioned multitudes their harps may tune,
And in their holy sanctity commune.

And see! here Mua comes! she stops and waits
Within a *gesdin* bower beside its gates. .
Around, above her spreads a flowering vine,
And o'er a ruby fountain almandine.
And on a graven garnet table grand,
Carved cups of solid pearl and tilpe stand.
A Zadu reservoir stands near, which rounds
The fount wherein the fragrant nectar bounds.
The ground is strewn with pari gems and pearls,
Wherefrom the light now softly backward hurls
Its rays o'er couches of paruti stone,
Soft cushioned, circling in the inner zone
Beside the shining kami-sadi way,
Where nectar fountains in their splendor play.

The path leads far along Life's beauteous stream,
That ever through this World of joy doth gleam.

And see! the hero comes! and now doth near
The maiden, where with Love she waits him here.
She flings a flowering garland, weaves it round
His form as he comes by! He turns around,
And she enwraps his breast and arms, and says:

"Dear Izdubar! and thus my lover strays!
I'll bind thee with this fragrant chain to keep
Thee ever by my side! thy pleasant sleep
Hath kept my lover from my side too long!"

"O thou sweet spirit, like a warbling song
Thy words are to my heart! I sought for thee,
And thy bright face and presence did not see;
I come to tell thee that I must return,
When from thy father all the past shall learn."

"And wilt thou go from me to earth again?
No! no! dear Izdubar, I thee enchain!"

"'Tis true, my love, I must return to men;
My duty calls me to my throne again."

"Dear Izdubar! my friend! my love! my heart!
I cannot let thee from my soul depart!
Thou shinest in my breast as some bright star!
And shall I let thee from me go afar?"

"But Mua, we immortal are, and we
There might return; and thou on earth shalt see
The glories of my kingdom,--be my queen!
Upon a couch I'll seat thee, there to reign
With me, my beauteous queen,--beside me sit;
And kings will come to us and kiss thy feet.
With all my wealth I'll clothe thee, ever love
Thee, fairest of these glorious souls that move
Within this Happy World. My people there
Shall love us,--ever drive away all care!"

When Mua heard him offer thus his hand,
She then unbinds him,--thoughtful now doth stand.

COLUMN VI

MUA'S ANSWER

Sweet Mua lifts her eyes toward the heights
That glow afar beneath the softened lights
That rest upon the mountain's crystalline.
And see! they change their hues incarnadine
To gold, and emerald, and opaline;
Swift changing to a softened festucine
Before the eye. And thus they change their hues
To please the sight of every soul that views
Them in that Land; but she heeds not the skies,
Or glorious splendor of her home; her eves
Have that far look of spirits viewing men
On earth, from the invisible mane,
That erstwhile rests upon the mortal eye,--
A longing for that home beyond the sky;

A yearning for that bliss that love imparts,
Where pain and sorrow reach no mortal hearts.

A light now breaks across her beauteous face;
She, turning, says to him with Heavenly grace:

"Dear Izdubar, thou knowest how I love
Thee, how my heart my love doth daily prove;
And, oh, I cannot let thee go alone.
I know not what awaits each soul there gone.
Our spirits often leave this glorious land,
Invisible return on earth, and stand
Amidst its flowerets, 'neath its glorious skies.
Thou knowest every spirit here oft flies
From earth, but none its secrets to us tell,
Lest some dark sorrow might here work its spell.
And, oh, I could not see dark suffering, woe
There spread, with power none to stop its flow!

I saw thee coming to us struck with fire,
Oh, how to aid thee did my heart desire!
Our tablets tell us how dread sorrow spreads
Upon that world and mars its glowing meads.
But, oh, so happy am I, here to know
That they with us here end all sorrow, woe.
O precious Izdubar! its sights would strike
Me there with sadness, and my heart would break!
And yet I learn that it is glorious, sweet!
To there enjoy its happiness,--so fleet

It speeds to sorrowing hearts to turn their tears
To joy! How sweet to them when it appears,
And sends a gleam of Heaven through their lives!

No! no! dear heart! I cannot go! It grieves
Thee! come, my dear one! quick to us return;
We here again will pair our love, and learn
How sweet it is to meet with joy again;
How happy will sweet love come to us then!"

She rests her head upon his breast, and lifts
Her face for Love's sweet kiss, and from them drifts
A halo o'er the shining gesdin-trees
And spreads around them Heaven's holy rays.
He her sweet lips, and brow, and eyes,
Then turns his gaze toward the glowing skies:

"I bless thee, for thy sweetest spirit here!
I bless this glorious land, that brings me near
To one that wafts sweet Heaven in my heart;
From thy dear plains how can my soul depart?
O Mua, Mua! how my heart now sings!
Thy love is sweeter than all earthly things!
I would I were not crowned a king!--away
From this bright land--here would I ever stay!
As thou hast said, I soon will here return;
The earth cannot withhold me from this bourne,
And soon my time allotted there will end,
And hitherward how happy I will wend!"

"And when thou goest, how my love shall there
Guard thee, and keep thy heart with Mua here.
Another kiss!"
               Her form doth disappear
Within the garden, gliding through the air.
He seats himself upon a couch and rests
His head upon his hand, and thought invests
Him round. His memory returns again
To Erech's throne, and all the haunts of men.
He rises, turns his footsteps to the halls,
And thoughtful disappears within its walls.

Printed in the USA
CPSIA information can be obtained
at www.ICGtesting.com
LVHW022155090324
774051LV00008B/889

9 781463 727550